Praise for Thom

"Tom's innovative approach to applying Outcome Driven Innovation and Jobs To Be Done theory to his Shot Calling framework will help anyone, at any level, move up the ladder and win more!"

—Anthony W. Ulwick
Founder and Chief Executive Officer of Strategyn, LLC, Author of
What Customers Want

"Putting words and concepts to the moving forces behind a solid go-to-market strategy is like lighting up the laws of physics while you're building a vessel to get to space. This is what Tom Miller's book on Shot Calling does for go-to-market strategy."

—Tamer Hassan
Co-Founder and Chief Executive Officer of White Ops

"Tom contributed significantly to the growth of Malwarebytes. His Shot Caller framework takes his strategies to the next level and will help any business move faster and win more!"

—Marcin Kleczynski
Co-Founder and Chief Executive Officer of Malwarebytes

"I've worked closely with Tom for many years creating winning strategies and growth. The Shot Caller framework captures so much of what it takes for a business to succeed. Tom's approach is useful and one of the essential considerations to unlock value".

—Lane Bess
Former Chief Executive Officer of Palo Alto Networks, Founder of
Bess Ventures and Advisory

"As a leading Silicon Valley executive coach, I see first and the challenges that derail businesses. Tom's Shot Calling approach offers a clear framework for understanding the reality of business success while providing powerful tools needed to create winning outcomes!"

—Mahbod Seraji
Executive Leadership Coach, Author of *Rooftops of Tehran*

CALL YOUR SHOTS

Gravity is infinite.
Innovation creates value.
Value creates mass.
Mass creates gravity.
Strategy is the altering of gravity to maximize your chances
of achieving your objective.

CALL YOUR SHOTS

A Uniquely Workable Approach for Demystifying the Universal Laws of Business, Creating Winning Strategy, Unlocking Value, Unifying Teams, Avoiding Peril, and Making You Unstoppable

THOMAS J. MILLER

INFA Advisors LLC
Bridgewater, NJ

INFA Advisors LLC

Bridgewater, NJ

www.ShotCallerSystem.com

Send feedback to Info@ShotCallerSystem.com

Printed in the United States of America

Publisher's Cataloging-In-Publication Data
(Prepared by The Donohue Group, Inc.)

Names: Miller, Thomas J. (Thomas James), 1961- author.

Title: Call your shots : a uniquely workable approach for demystifying the universal laws of business, creating winning strategy, unlocking value, unifying teams, avoiding peril, and making you unstoppable / Thomas J. Miller.

Description: Bridgewater, New Jersey : INFA Advisors LLC, [2020] | Includes bibliographical references.

Identifiers: ISBN 9781735790602 (paperback) | ISBN 9781735790619 (hardback) | ISBN 9781735790626 (ebook)

Subjects: LCSH: Success in business. | Management--Employee participation. | Organizational effectiveness. | Strategic planning. | Teams in the workplace.

Classification: LCC HF5386 .M55 2020 (print) | LCC HF5386 (ebook) | DDC 650.1--dc23

Special discounts for bulk sales are available.

Please contact Info@ShotCallerSystem.com.

For all my wonderful family, friends, and colleagues who helped and supported me during this journey, thank you all. I am so very grateful for your advice, feedback, and the occasional bullshit you called that helped inspire me to do my very best. I hope my endeavor is worthy of your gravity. You are all Shot Callers to me.

Contents

FOREWORD

By Mahbod Seraji

I've known Tom for many years and have had the pleasure of working with him in multiple settings. We bonded immediately as we shared a passion—finding the clearest path to growing a company. We discussed our ideas at work or over a cup of coffee or a glass of wine. We argued over the available methods, the application of each, examples of where they led to success or flopped. We talked about how businesses failed, why they failed, and how they could have avoided their fate. We agreed that for the most part, businesses don't fail, people do. People who fail to make the right decisions for their businesses.

This idea, Shot-Calling, constitutes the core of Tom's model. Once he explained it to me, I pictured a coach observing the field of play, or a general commanding a battlefield, assessing the strengths and advantages on both sides, and calling in the right plays and moves. Tom's Shot Calling is an exceptionally practical model for creating, replicating, and sustaining a winning strategy. So much of what I see as an executive coach is how fragile business really is, and how quickly things can get off track. The framework Tom uses teaches readers how business is interconnected, how winning really happens, and how its perils can be avoided. He breaks his framework into a sequence that begins the first principle ideas that form the basis of success. He then explains the interconnection of the shots that make winning possible. The Moonshot teaches shot callers to identify forces that support or work against their business and how they can be manipulated for success. This, Tom calls, "gravity," and his model explores ways those gravitational forces serve as an advantage or a deterrence to an enterprise. The tools Tom introduces, help practitioners understand these forces, and chart the strategy for success. In the next step, the Kill Shot, Tom teaches us how to turn strategy into action by revealing the truth that 70 percent of the value of any offer comes from the inner core. Understanding how to package your inner core is of immense value in this section of the book. He provides the tools that enable you to maximize the value of your offerings in the buyers' mind.

The Money Shot, the Three-Point Shot, and the Whole Shot provide frameworks for how to replicate success, how to be a great leader, and how to unify the team. In each section, Tom provides prescriptive tips on how to allow shot-callers to make the right calls.

The book is full of wonderful examples, and interesting stories of success and failures. Tom's passion for winning shows on every page, and in the way, he tells each story. This is not a theoretical book, filled with untested ideas and unproven formulas. This is a book for practitioners, for people in the trenches, for people who have made difficult decisions every day. This is a well-written, brief book with real examples, useful models, and easy-to-use tools that promise to transform your business. Tom told me once that he seeks to democratize power with the Shot Calling System and help everyone, at every level, to be successful. This book delivers on that promise.

—**Mahbod Seraji**
Executive Leadership Coach,
Author of *Rooftops of Tehran*

INTRODUCTION

Are You a Kabuki Dancer or a Shot Caller?

In early 2003, I had my first meeting with Steve Chang, the founder and CEO of Trend Micro. I joined Trend Micro after a prosperous run as a sales rep and sales manager at large companies and startups you've never heard of. Cybersecurity (no one called it that at the time) was in its infancy, and I was eager to make my mark. I was also eager to make a good impression on Steve since he could make or break my future with the company.

Steve was in town with my boss at the time, Lane Bess, who eventually became the CEO of Palo Alto Networks. Steve and Lane wanted to check out Trend Micro's new East Coast operations office, so I met them there.

I felt nervous about meeting Steve. He had a reputation for being impulsive. I'd heard he once decided in the middle of a conference he was attending in Hawaii that he needed to visit the world's first six-star hotel, which had just opened in Dubai. Steve left. No flight booked. No reservation at the hotel. He didn't even pack. He just told his handler they needed to leave. Twenty-four hours later they're checked into the Burj Al Arab. Steve buys some clothes, they stay for one day, and guess what? Steve decides it's time to leave—again without his clothes. So you can imagine my trepidation at meeting someone like Steve.

I arrived at the office and the three of us sat down. After some pleasantries, Steve turned to me.

"So, Tom, what makes you so good at sales?"

They say that life comes down to a few critical moments. This was one for me. Knowing Steve's reputation, I decided to be bold.

"I don't suffer from sacrifice-the-virgin syndrome," I replied. Did I really say that? Damn right I did.

Lane looked at me like I was mentally ill. Steve just stared at me. After a long pause, Steve said, "What the hell is sacrifice-the-virgin syndrome?"

"It's what the Aztecs did to gain the favor of the gods," I said, trying to keep my cool. "Bad weather? Kill a virgin. Too many enemies? Kill a virgin. Plague, disease, locusts, you name it—kill a virgin. You get the idea."

"But what does that have to do with being good at sales?" Steve asked.

"Steve, most people don't have a clue why things turn out the way they do. They shake their asses at something, and if something good happens they take the credit. But if something bad happens, they find the next virgin to kill. I don't play that game. I know why things turn out the way they do. I call my own shots. Most other people are just guessing."

Steve paused again. Finally, he asked, "Why a virgin? Why not a chicken or a goat?"

Lane laughed in relief. Steve had a good sense of humor. He didn't fire me. He understood where I was coming from. He even wanted to know more.

Steve is the most engaging force of nature I've ever met. He doesn't speak perfect English, but put him in front of a thousand English-speaking people and he'll mesmerize every one of them.

Years later, Steve graciously invited me to join him for a seminar at MIT led by Peter Senge, author of *The Fifth Discipline*. In that diverse group of professionals from all around the world, as always, Steve owned the room.

Steve is unique. He built a billion-dollar company with his instincts, his intelligence, and his energy—which is nearly limitless. I'm not Steve. You're not Steve. So what does this have to do with you?

That first meeting with Steve was the beginning of my pursuit of the truth about cause and effect in business. I'd already mastered it from a sales perspective, but I wanted to master it comprehensively. Fortunately, Trend Micro and Steve's successor as CEO, Eva Chen, gave me the chance to do that. I've spent the last fifteen years learning and applying theories, frameworks, best practices, and my own hard-earned experiences to reach the conclusions you're going to read about.

I've worked with some amazing people and some genuine assholes. I've been promoted, and I've been fired. I've had many wins and some tough losses. This is what I've learned, boiled down into one sentence: unless you can call your own shots, you're the problem. If you're not calling your own shots, you're just a Kabuki Dancer. In business, nothing is more dangerous or loathsome than a Kabuki Dancer.

What's a Kabuki Dancer, you ask? In classical Japanese Kabuki theater, the acting, costumes, and dance are largely for effect. The movements of a Kabuki Dancer may look flashy, but that's all they are. There's no actual point beyond your entertainment. The people I refer to as Kabuki Dancers in business are all skilled at sacrificing virgins. Their bluster, histrionics, proclamations, prodding, pleading, threatening, and reorganizing are nothing more than melodramatic attempts to cover up the truth: they don't know what the hell they're doing.

Let me be clear—I don't blame the Kabuki Dancers who just don't know any better. I do blame those who *know* they're Kabuki Dancers and refuse to learn to be Shot Callers. Screw them. I know I sound bitter. I'm not. I'm incredibly hopeful that I can help *any* business professional who wants to avoid Kabuki dancing and learn how to call their own shots.

To that end, this book highlights the five shots you must call if you're going to win in business. Actually win. Not "win" at a stupid game like playing politics. Each shot is a critical element of business success. Mastering them will be key to your personal success just as it's been to mine. Each shot requires thoughtfulness and dedication. I've learned, practiced, and taken all of them over the course of my entire career. They are:

1. **Moonshot**—How do you unlock value, avoid peril, and create winning strategy?

2. **Kill Shot**—Are you making and keeping the right promises to customers?

3. **Money Shot**—How do you plan for success and win more?

4. **Three-Point Shot**—How do you help teammates take and make the big shot?

5. **Whole Shot**—Can you get no-BS buy-in from everyone who matters?

Why these five shots? Simple. In my thirty-five years in business, I've always felt frustrated that no one could explain what matters to achieve desirable outcomes in a comprehensive, cohesive, yet concise manner. So that's what I will attempt to do for you. My goal is for this book to be your go-to resource for understanding business so you can move faster with confidence and win more, whatever your role at your company looks like. I also hope it restores some of the integrity to both corporate and startup culture that Kabuki Dancers have damaged. This book is about commitment to excellence. There are no shortcuts here. Success is hard. So unless you're blessed with some Jedi mind trick ability to use "the Force" on colleagues, customers, and competitors, this book is for you.

Let's briefly examine the five shots you'll learn to call, what they address, and the work you must do for each one. You need to know something first: if you can't take and make all five shots in sequence, you are *not* a Shot Caller. There are a million books written on each of the five shots separately. And that's the problem. You can be an expert in one shot, but that doesn't mean shit; if you get the other four wrong, you're going to fail.

The Five Shots to Call in Business

Moonshot

The Moonshot encompasses the most strategic decisions you'll ever make. Businesses pay consulting firms hundreds of thousands of dollars to answer these questions. What are your vision and mission? What *should* they be? And how do you define them in one hour?

What about strategy? What is your objective, scope, and uniqueness? And how do you describe all of these in a single succinct strategy statement? Well, these are ultimately determined by your core value, which I refer to as your *mass*. So what is your mass?

In the Moonshot chapter, I'll borrow the theory of gravity to show you the fastest, simplest, and *only* right way to call your Moonshot. Why gravity? Because nature solves problems. Humans should copy its answers. For example, nature solved the problem of how to organize the universe; physical reality is largely organized by gravity. The theory of gravity takes into account how much mass something has. Is it so heavy it can create some form of attraction? What's the business application of Moonshot theory? Customer attraction, of course. I use the quasi-metaphor "business gravity" to explain how to apply each step of the Moonshot in sequence to progressively organize everything your business does to attract customers and keep them in your orbit.

Kill Shot

If you're a marketer, you might as well change the name of what you do from marketing to proximity—moving closer to your customers. The job of marketing is to effect outcomes through proximity. The desired valuable and underserved outcomes create your best opportunities. To seize those opportunities, you've got a few questions to answer. How do you define and defend your value stack proposition? What's your short-cut for helping customers understand your value stack proposition—your brand promise?

The Kill Shot isn't a silver bullet. It's about putting the right tip on the spear of your marketing. It's how your core value penetrates the market. So what is your core value? Does your buyer value function? Emotion? Are they obsessed with status? Do they want to brag about how they stood in line, got their iPhone with three cameras before you did, and can say, "I'm great, you suck; I win, you lose"? That's half the iPhone customer base.

This talk of outcomes, iPhones, and jobs to be done doesn't mean this book is about the innovation process. The best innovation system is called Outcome-Driven Innovation® (ODI). I am a big fan of ODI, which was pioneered by Tony Ulwick. Everyone should read his book *What Customers Want*. Many of those principles underpin my conclusions. The premise of ODI is to create tools to help customers get jobs done. And when they have a new job to get done, even a bad tool is going to be successful because a bad tool is better than no tool. As the customer gets the job done, then the question is, can you help them get the job done better? The Kill Shot chapter reveals the answer.

In the Kill Shot chapter, I'm going to give you the prescription to reveal your value in the best possible light. I'll help you answer the essential questions that will set you up for success. For example, who is your target buyer? How are you going to use proximity strategies to get closer to them? How are you precisely locking on to your target customer and reaching as many of them as effectively as possible with the right offer—a new, better way to get the job done? And how are you going to identify what they value? Nobody can simply guess the right answers. They take a lot of work and much thought. For example, what's the most valuable feature of an iPhone? Is it the battery life? The brightness of the screen? The quality of the speaker? Is it one camera? Is it two cameras? Three cameras? Is it the antenna? There are so many jobs that people are trying to get done with an iPhone. When it comes to your solution, how do you separate the valuable ones from the ones buyers don't care that much about?

Notice I said *solution*, not *product*. You've probably heard of the Four *P*s of marketing: product, placement, price, promotion. The Kill Shot replaces that outdated approach with the acronym SAVE, which is all about proximity. It stands for solution, access, value, and education. Why do I use SAVE over the Four *P*s? Because you don't market your product, you highlight how it's a solution. You don't think about placement, you focus on how customers can access the solution. You don't tell people about price first, you talk about value. And you don't do promotion—you don't put stuff on sale to hook impulse buyers who will never use it. You *educate*.

There's a lot to cover related to the Kill Shot, but by the end of the chapter you'll be the best damn marketing and sales strategist your company has—even if your job isn't marketing or you've never written a word of sales copy in your life. If you can make a business impact, you'll help yourself move up in salary and responsibility. That's how it works. Don't work an eight-to-five? If you run your own business, you have to know how to take out your competitors ethically with proximity so that nothing—no other product, no pitch, no ad—can get between you and your customers.

Money Shot

I've been taking the Money Shot for three and a half decades. Let me tell you something I've learned. Sales is the most noble profession there is. It's also the loneliest. Everyone wants to be in sales until they try it. Leaders love a salesperson when they're selling; they might as well not exist when they aren't. The good news is that success is a planned event. The Money Shot is designed to make one of the hardest jobs in the world easier. To sell more is a goal; to consistently meet and even exceed quota is a system. In the Money Shot, you learn that system. Specifically, you're going to learn productivity modeling and money mapping, which together enable you to forecast sales, scale your production, and figure out what to do if you're not performing at desired levels.

I'll also guide you through designing your own execution workflow, which describes who does what and when during the customer life cycle. This covers everything from marketing communication and "cradle-to-grave" sales strategy to the separation of duties between marketing and sales so everyone can execute effectively and make their numbers.

Kabuki dancing with any of these numbers and variables is prohibited. Speaking of which, you've probably heard that sales is a numbers game, which is true, but Shot Callers will go further. That's what my reframing of sales as a symbols game does: it builds on the Moonshot and Kill Shot chapters to show where to focus and how to win. A major variable in this is what I call the highest level of strategic intersection. It's the one reason above all others that motivates someone to buy. In the Money Shot, I'll show you how to find it. Even if you're a newly hired individual contributor.

Now, what if you're not in sales? Is the Money Shot relevant? You bet it is, and here's why: The Money Shot determines everyone's fate, not just those in sales. Even if you don't carry a quota or touch a P&L statement in your daily job, you'll be significantly more valuable if you understand how to help move the needle.

Three-Point Shot

I studied culture and leadership at MIT and Harvard. That makes what I'm going to say next so surprising: You can't create an awesome culture by working on culture. Instead, you have to create a framework for how your business intends to succeed. A system for business success is what's needed. I offer the Shot Calling system because it works. Once you have a company full of Shot Callers, everyone feels like they're in a company where the culture is a Shot-Caller culture. It will just happen.

Kabuki Dancers talk about culture. Shot Callers hire Shot Callers and thus create a culture of Shot Callers. Most advice about culture has this exactly backward. In reality, the system dictates the culture. Because the system *is* the culture. Put Shot Callers in every office, every conference room, every cubicle, every home office, and you've got a Shot-Caller culture. But send surveys and hang inspirational quotes on the walls, and you don't have a culture, you have a bonfire of egos, power, platitudes, and ping pong tables. None of which moves the needle.

If three hundred people at your company became fitness freaks, you wouldn't sit around building a bunch of employee surveys about fitness. You wouldn't put up a bunch of posters about the virtue of fitness. And you for damn sure wouldn't walk around telling everyone, "Hey, we embrace a culture of fitness." All empty words. Instead, imagine that every day three hundred people go to the gym, work out, and eat healthy. What matters more? Promoting a culture of fitness or the fact that you have three hundred ass-kickers instinctively staying fit because they are following a system?

That said, even Shot-Caller cultures experience tension. Tension occurs when change stretches or strains the people in a company. Healthy tension is necessary; unhealthy tension kills companies. How can you tell the difference? And how do you manage tension in order to leave the current state of uncertainty and reach a more desirable state? We'll cover these in the Three-Point Shot chapter as well as the best way to think about becoming a good leader, which is the Three-Point Shot itself—the intersection of capability, passion, and value.

Whole Shot

Why are businesses failing? They can't call shots. They don't know how to do a Moonshot or a Kill Shot. They get the Money Shot wrong. They screw up the Three-Point Shot. Then they tie together all of those mistakes in an operating plan, business plan, or strategy execution plan, and they've got themselves a blueprint for failure.

In the Whole Shot, you put everything together into an operating plan. You'll confirm with every department and every person in your business that they're signing up for the mission. Is everybody down? Yeah, we're down. You're down, marketing team. Are you going to do these proximity moves? Yes. Product team, are you going to add this feature to increase the mass of value? Yes. Sales team, are you going to execute it?

Why call it the Whole Shot? In motorsports, the "holeshot" describes the racer or rider who gets up to speed and reaches the first turn before anyone else. Win the holeshot, and you have a massive advantage. It's an advantage that demoralizes the competition. In business, the Whole Shot implies that the entire organization is firing on all cylinders. You work like a pit crew. Before anyone sees what happened, you've all got the job done, from designing all four shots together and implementing them to winning big and being unstoppable. If you want to go fast, take the holeshot. If you want to go far, go together—that's the Whole Shot.

In the documentary series *Apollo*, there's a cool scene where everyone at NASA is going through the countdown. "Go life support, go mission control, go landing, go lunar . . . go, go, go, go." In seven seconds, seven department heads have one second to say go or no-go. Watch the look on their faces—this is life or death. Yes or no. Nobody says, "Well, I'll get back to you." No, it's time. You've got to go.

That's what happens in the final shot. It's not only important that you can put together an operating plan; can you get everybody on board? Do all stakeholders say yes? Once you get the mission locked, it's off to the races. It's called interlocking a plan. You're binding your strategy, product-level forecast, roadmap, and marketing and sales plan across functions in your organization. You can only get there if you're looking at your company top down and bottom up; what are the C-level and board targets, and how do those compare to the reality on the ground? If you can do that, you're officially a Shot Caller.

To help you get there, I'm going to teach you by example. Most stories throughout this book come from my career at some of the largest and most successful technology businesses at all stages of growth and at all levels of revenue. There's something here for you whether you're in software or insurance sales, whether you work for the Fortune 500 or are a solopreneur bootstrapping a business with a hundred bucks. What you will *not* find is another Kabuki Dancer's opinion. Everything you are reading about is what has survived my own extreme prejudice against what doesn't work. There is no pride of authorship, what matters is what works.

I apply that standard to my own ideas. The five shots you're learning rely on are strategies built on my thirty-five years of experience, twenty thousand–plus sales calls, elite business training, the award-winning business authors whose ideas helped make me rich, the three successful initial public offerings (IPOs) I've been a part of, and the company I recently left—which sold for 14 times annual revenue. If calling your shots didn't work, I would have gotten fired, I'd be broke, and I'd have nowhere to hide. But it does work. It works for me, and it will work for you in whatever job you have too.

Who Is Shot Calling For?

Depending on your role and your viewpoint, this book will be valuable to you in different ways. You may need to focus on two or three of the five shots, or you may need to master them all. I'm going to tell you exactly how to use this book according to the position you hold. The following functional guidance and commentary come from my experiences either managing or interacting with the following people with these titles. I've been in nearly every operating role in business.

Sales

This book can help you immensely. You take the bullets, absorb the heat, and often stand knee-deep in the shit that Kabuki Dancers produce. The Money Shot will be of special interest to you, especially if you're managing people. Learn all five shots (that's how I became an executive) and demand that your company be committed to excellence. Hold everyone around you accountable because you're screwed if you don't.

Marketing

You're our best hope—but you need to get off the fence. Most companies (especially in tech) don't win because they have the best product or they outsell competitors. They out-market them by developing strategies necessary to reveal inner core value and create demand for their product. This is never safe. Sitting on the fence trying to be everything to everybody is the worst mistake you can make. You own the Kill Shot and probably own the Moonshot—or at least have a lot to say about it.

Product and Engineering

You're the most important part of value creation. Great marketing can subsidize value deficits for a while, but not forever. You may be using great frameworks like Pragmatic and Agile, but you still need a Moonshot and a Kill Shot. These have to come from you. Anyone on a product team must master the Moonshot and understand antigravity. You won't achieve excellence without it.

HR, Finance, Legal, or Support

Demand that your organization produce a Three-Point Shot. Too many times I've seen the functions of the Three-Point Shot disconnected from the core of a business. If that's the case at your organization, it's not your fault. It's the fault of leadership. It's up to leadership to produce and communicate the Three-Point Shot for the rest of the organization. It's up to you to participate in the creation of all the shots so you can add gravity to the business. Otherwise, even your best efforts can reduce gravity instead of increasing it.

The CFO

You must hold the product, marketing, and sales teams accountable for the shots they call and the results they produce. That's the difference between a true CFO and a "finance guy." It's often amazing how obvious the lapses in value creation are but how indifferently CFOs react to them. You're the protector of more than just the bottom line. You protect the integrity of your company's performance. Embrace it.

The CEO, the Board, and VCs

There's a chance that you've built something so incredibly valuable that value creation and extraction strategies don't matter. If that's you, congratulations! Put down this book and enjoy Camelot! But it's not likely. Or maybe you've got a legitimate unicorn leading your company—the next Bill Gates, a true legend in the making. But there have been fewer than ten of those (at least in tech) in the last thirty years, so odds are you don't have one.

Most likely, the company you lead, direct, or fund needs to learn to execute all five shots. You need to learn them all if you don't already know them. Be a Shot Caller, not a Kabuki Dancer. Hold your team accountable for producing the deliverables associated with each shot. Use the shots to get everyone on the same page and build a culture that creates and rewards excellence. You'll be glad you did.

THE MOONSHOT

In February 2007, Eva Chen, the CEO of Trend Micro, invited me to lunch. At the time, I was running Trend Micro North American Sales. We took a break from the RSA Conference (an information security product trade show) and met at the W Hotel.

As we sat down for lunch, the first words out of her mouth were, "I want you to be the general manager (GM) of the enterprise segment."

I was stunned. Trend Micro had restructured business sales several years earlier (more on that later). The GMs of consumer, small and medium-size business (SMB) and enterprise ran their respective business units like CEOs. In the enterprise segment, this meant running an engineering team of five hundred developers and architects; a marketing team of product managers, product marketers, and "line of business" executives; and the staff necessary to create and execute on strategy, roadmap, and go-to-market with a $400 million P&L. Six hundred people in total.

I'd never written a line of code, launched a product, or run an engineering organization. I replied to Eva's offer logically: "Are you crazy?"

"I don't think so." She smiled. "I want to put you in this role because enterprise isn't reflecting the voice of the customer in the market. Your track record in sales distinguishes you. Your teams are selling more than the other teams."

"Thank you, but—"

"You've got your finger on the pulse of the marketplace. You're on the front line, and you're winning. All you have to do is transform your knowledge and understanding of customers into strategy, roadmap, and go-to-market for the enterprise segment."

Eva's offer—and my eventual acceptance—began the value creation stage of my career. No way could I succeed if I didn't figure out every aspect of value creation. I couldn't Kabuki dance my way to success. So I became a sponge and consumed as much material as I could on the subject. I hired the Chasm Group, a leading strategy consulting company, and began my journey. Over the course of the next ten years, I arrived at the following immutable business truth: **Companies get what they deserve**. Or, put into context, **if you don't build your Moonshot properly, you're screwed.**

Let's get two things out of the way right now. One, this book is not about the innovation process. (Read *What Customers Want* to learn how to innovate.) I'm assuming your innovation process is already in place. Two, the Moonshot doesn't matter if you don't have the money to execute. I'm assuming that you have reasonable access to the capital needed to call your shots.

I like to think of the Moonshot as **the intersection of imagination and committed endeavor**. It's a dream so worth following that you actually do it. President John F. Kennedy burned the word into our lexicon with this profound description:

> We choose to go to the moon. We choose to go to the moon in this decade and do the other things, not because they are easy, but because they are hard, because that goal will serve to organize and measure the best of our energies and skills, because that challenge is one that we are willing to accept, one we are unwilling to postpone, and one which we intend to win, and the others, too.[1]

Putting a man on the moon was JFK's committed endeavor—the thing so worth doing that it got done. So what is the Moonshot, and what does it have to do with value creation, strategy, and the no-screwing-around reasons you're in business? I'm glad you asked.

---

1   "JFK Rice Moon Speech." NASA. Accessed September 1, 2020. https://er.jsc.nasa.gov/seh/ricetalk.htm.

Introduction to Moonshooting

Before you get started building your Moonshot, you must learn what makes it possible. This puts you on the path to become a Shot Caller. The sequence of these concepts may not seem natural at first, but the Moonshot is invaluable. I will teach you the components of the Moonshot, but you must put your skin in the game.

Ever heard the expression "burn the boats"? I love it. The story goes that when Viking leaders landed in a new world, they would immediately set their boats on fire. I picture one Viking whispering to another, "Oh shit, how do we get back?" and the other saying, "I guess there's no going back." My point? Burn your boats because there's no going back.

To be a Shot Caller, you must master all the components of the Moonshot, which are:

- Value creation
- Value type
- Mass
- Value stacking
- Gravity
- Vision
- Mission
- Strategy

To demonstrate your mastery of these components, you will produce the following deliverables:

- Vision statement
- Mission statement
- Value stack
- Whole Shot Grid

When you have written these four deliverables, you will have successfully built your Moonshot. Trust me for now that this is the sequence you must follow. You'll understand completely by the end of this chapter when your Moonshot is complete. Kabuki Dancers either can't produce these deliverables, or they make them so unrealistic that they're actually destructive. So pay close attention and don't screw them up.

Let's deconstruct the Moonshot components one by one. It's essential that you understand them. If you do, you'll benefit from your Moonshot for the rest of your career. Also, I've racked my brain over this stuff for years, so I'll be pissed if you half-ass it:

Value (and Its Components)

Before you can work on vision, mission, and strategy, you must learn the components of value. After you understand value, creating vision, mission, and strategy will be *much* easier! Let's get into them.

Innovation is **value creation**. This is pretty straightforward. Something gets built, constructed, coded, baked, filmed, bottled, manufactured, packaged, or written (like this book). Then you extract value from it in the form of an offer, i.e., a product or service.

Your offer's value is always perceived in three **value types—functional value, emotional value,** and **economic value**. Humans always perceive value as a combination of these three value types. This *never* changes. Anytime value is exchanged, both parties are perceiving the worthiness of the exchange as a combination of *all* three forms of value. Not all three value types are perceived equally, which is why it is critical to understand how to stack your value stack proposition.

Mass is the amount of value your offer creates. The more value something has, the greater its mass. Big Value = Big Mass. Small Value = Small Mass. In an ideal world, your offer has "mass out the ass." Remember, the mass of your offer consists of those three types of value—functional, emotional, and economic.

Value stacking establishes which value type (functional, emotional, or economic) your offer contains the most of (the "inner core"), which it contains the second most of (the "outer core"), and which it contains the least of (the "mantle"). Remember, every offer is perceived as having all three types of value, but no two value stacks are exactly the same. The coolest part of knowing your value stack is using it to guide your entire business strategy, which you'll learn about shortly.

Gravity is everything.

Now, this is where I need you to suspend disbelief for a moment and accept that the following is true: *Value doesn't exist.* Value is only *perceived* in the minds of humans. No humans, no value. While we spend so much of our lives "valuing" relationships, possessions, experiences, choices, careers, and so on, the only way we talk about value is price. But price is just a reflection of what we think something is worth. We need a better way to talk about value. So here it is.

Value is a fabric with three dimensions, just like the fabric of space. Anything of value forms a dent in that fabric the same way anything with mass forms a dent in the fabric of space. As we know, a dent in space creates gravity. In the Moonshot, we're simply extending this metaphor to the value of your offer. Your offer has mass that creates gravity. In physics and in business, Big Mass = Big Gravity. Small Mass = Small Gravity.

Value behaves like gravity. If you understand gravitational theory from a scientific perspective, you will understand the Moonshot. I've tried explaining the Moonshot to people without the gravity metaphor, but it falls flat. Here's why: This whole discussion is a metaphor! Value is an abstract concept that only exists the moment a human perceives its existence. No matter how anyone describes these concepts, they're using metaphors, comparisons, and analogies. For example, value doesn't actually "migrate" or "flow." It's not a herd of wildebeest, and it's not a river. So as long as any discussion about value is going to be a metaphor, I'm going to use the one that's most useful—gravity. You'll find it useful for the rest of your life and beyond.

So let's talk about gravity. Gravitational force is created by an object with mass. Everything that has mass has gravity. You, this book, and the laptop I typed this on. The more mass, the more gravity. Get used to this analogy, as it's essential throughout the book. The better your innovation, the bigger the core, the more value it holds, and the more gravity it creates. Just as mass creates a dent in the fabric of space, the core creates a dent in the fabric of value. So core equals gravity. Big core, big gravity. Small core, small gravity.

Then introduce a second object and think of that as your target customer. Assume the first object is your offer with the core at the center, and the second object is your customer. But just as the universe doesn't have one object with mass creating all gravity, the marketplace doesn't have one offer with mass creating all gravity either. Mass is the starting point for how much gravity your offer creates. Are we stuck with winning or losing based on how much gravity our offer's mass creates? No! The concept of gravity actually breaks down into four different types of gravity, where each can be manipulated independent of the others. Within this manipulation lies the key to your success.

Learning to manipulate gravity allows you to design winning strategies wherever you go. That's all strategy is, really: altering business gravity to maximize your chances of success. So how do you manipulate gravity?

The Four Types of Gravity

Strategy is the altering of gravity to maximize your chances of success. Altering gravity is merely knowing which gravity types you have to account for and then using them as "gravity levers" to get your desired outcome.

(And for any straight-A physics students, yes, I know you never read "gravity type" in a textbook. The metaphor's components are not scientifically precise, which isn't my point anyway. If you want to learn rocket science, you're in the wrong place. This book is for creating Shot Callers, and the gravity metaphor is good enough to turn you into one. Disclaimer aside, let's now examine the four types of gravity.)

Mass

You know that mass is the amount of value created by your offer. The more mass your offer has, the stronger its gravity. Need to attract more customers? Simple. Add more mass. And since mass is created by value, you should be doing everything you can to add more value to your offer before you start talking to customers about it. Many companies would think of this as their product roadmap.

Proximity

Let's time travel back to high school. As you might remember, in physics, you calculate gravity by looking at the mass of an object (planet, star, comet, etc.) and its *proximity* to other objects. If you want your object to have more gravity, you *could* double its mass. Or you could just shorten the proximity, moving your object twice as close to the object. The second one is a hell of a lot less work.

That's what proximity is in business. Your gravity increases when you move your offer closer to your target customer in order to create higher perceived value. Think of this on a scale where the goal is to establish the appropriate level of intimacy with your target customer. Enterprises demand high levels of intimacy (more proximity) and smaller businesses will accept less intimacy (less proximity). Proximity is anything you do *once* you start communicating with the market. Many companies would refer to this as their "go-to-market" strategy. Oftentimes, it's more effective to alter gravity using proximity strategy instead of altering mass. Why waste time and money making your mass bigger when you can simply reduce the distance between you and your customer? Of course, you want your offer to be as massive as possible, but no matter what, moving a valuable offer closer to customers will increase their attraction to it.

Opposing Gravity

As you might guess, opposing gravity refers to the gravity of your customers' best alternative to your offer, including the massive opposing gravity of your customer simply doing nothing. The status quo has "mass out the ass." What amount of value (i.e., mass and therefore gravity) does your customer think the best alternative to your offer has? The answer will give you an accurate sense of how much opposing gravity you face. You *must* use the Opposing Gravity Grid (fig. 1.1) because you *must* account for opposing gravity in your strategy using antigravity. Antigravity strategies are designed to deplete the mass of your customers' next best alternative. Done with enough effort, they are powerful.

I know, I know. "Don't bash the competition." That advice is bullshit. Your competition directs their gravity toward your target customer all the time. They may not disparage your offer in overt ways, but they're going after your customers nonetheless. There are no rules for applying antigravity. The only thing you don't want is antitrust (funny how antitrust sounds like antigravity), so just don't lose your target customer's trust. Other than that, game on.

Antigravity can be just as powerful as positive gravity, so take advantage of it. How? With the Opposing Gravity Grid. You will use this grid again once you create your antigravity strategy. For now, focus on a hypothesis inspired by the book *What Customers Want*, which explains that products are tools to help customers get jobs done. This simple yet powerful idea has guided me for years, and it will guide our understanding of opposing gravity as well. Here's how.

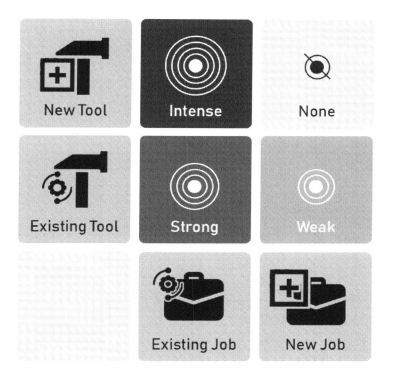

Figure 1.1 The Opposing Gravity Grid.

Here's how to use the Opposing Gravity Grid. It's easy.

- Are you offering customers a **New Tool** for an **Existing Job**? You will face **intense** gravity from competitors. That's because anyone facing the threat of a new tool disrupting their gravity has no choice but to react in the most intense possible way in order to preserve their value.
- Are you offering customers an **Existing Tool** for an **Existing Job**? You will face **strong** gravity from competitors. That's because anyone facing the threat of another competitor of equal

gravity will fight back—but not as intensely as for a new tool because the threat is not as great.

- Are you offering customers a **New Tool** for a **New Job**? You will face virtually **no** gravity from competitors. That's because there is zero gravity coming from alternatives that don't exist.
- Are you offering customers an **Existing Tool** for a **New Job**? You will face **weak** gravity from competitors. That's because there is some, albeit limited, gravity coming from alternatives.

Super Gravity

Super gravity occurs when the strength of gravity increases disproportionately to the resources invested. The three forms of super gravity are network effect, delayed reward, and value chain. That's it. But more details to come about this.

Shot Callers are gravity gods. They manipulate gravity for their own purposes, setting up the profoundly important relationship between gravity and strategy. Here's the deal: Strategy is simply altering gravity to maximize your chances of success. This is a profoundly superior definition of strategy, one you must accept if you're going to become a Shot Caller.

Orbit

Orbit is what happens when your strategy works. It's the balance that occurs when two objects are the right distance apart. A satellite in Earth's orbit is going to stay there, going around and around us as long as it's needed. In our metaphor, orbit is not a form of gravity but an indication of whether or not there is gravity and how strong it is. In a business context, orbit refers to *appropriately* serving your customer. When you decide to *over*serve or *under*serve your customers, you fall out of orbit. Achieve orbit, and you create a win-win situation between you and your target customer.

Orbit is a diagnostic tool. If you don't have orbit, it tells you that the existing strategy has not worked or it confirms that your decision to overserve or underserve your target market is working. Ultimately, you will want to *appropriately* serve your target market. This means a healthy margin and a growing or least stable business. However, many companies—especially early stage tech companies—chose to overserve their target market as a way to grab market share. Once they reach a dominant position, then they start milking more profits from their offer.

Conversely, other businesses, like hospitals, decide to strategically underserve the market. Any company without competition and with a lot of customers isn't going anywhere. You can enjoy more profit than growth. You don't have many options to add mass, so you're living off the fat of the land. Are you willing to overserve the market to win, like Tesla or ZScaler? Can you get to the Promised Land before you run out of money?

We're going to take a brief detour into an area that seems to have nothing to do with value or business gravity. I promise this twofold topic will come up again, if for no other reason than the fact that every company I've ever worked for has expected me to take a position on it. Although that's not the only reason.

That essential topic is vision and mission. What do a company's vision and mission statements have to do with strategy? Nothing—at least not at the outset of your Moonshot. Later, when you're designing your Moonshot strategy to bring customers into orbit and keep them there, vision and mission serve a brief but important purpose. Together, they confirm you have an "all- systems-are-go" strategy—or they alert you to something wrong before blastoff. For now, the important point is that you learn how to write your vision and mission.

Vision: Aspirational Good

You're not alone if you've gotten stuck here before. I've grinded on vision statements for days. The fate of the company seems to hang on every word. But don't overthink vision. And don't Kabuki dance its value. It is *not* that important. Vision statements merely capture the aspirational good that an organization hopes to deliver. At Trend Micro, we envisioned "a world safe for the exchange of digital information." At Malwarebytes, we said, "We believe everyone has the fundamental right to a malware-free existence."

These visions provide a North Star to keep everyone going in the right direction. Supposedly, they inspire us to work harder by reinforcing the good we bring to society. But I can confirm that in the ten years I spent on the executive teams at those two companies, vision statements never really mattered. While they are useful for giving a sense of direction, they rarely impact reality on the ground. That's what separates vision from mission.

When you create your vision statement, don't make it inconsistent with your business aspirations. I like Google's vision statement, which is "to provide access to the world's information in one click." No Kabuki dancing there. It's what Google has been saying since their inception. They're organizing the world's data, and now they want you to have access to it in one click. It's great for customers, it's great for Google, and it's bad for competitors. Now that's a vision!

Your aspirational good and your desired outcome must be consistent. Let's use George W. Bush's "war on terror" as an example. If you were in the business of defeating terrorism, your vision is "a world free from terrorism." This statement speaks to the aspirational good, and it's consistent with the desired outcome. Eliminating terrorism is good for society, *and* it's good for the governments, militaries, and law enforcement bodies that all succeed if the vision is realized. You could include a time boundary here, like "within a generation," but it's not essential. Vision statements need to express a win-win sentiment. If yours doesn't, keep working on it until it does.

If someone tells you your vision should be purely aspirational, meaning never achieved but only relentlessly pursued, don't listen to them. No one gives a shit about a vision they can't imagine being realized.

Mission: Committed Endeavor

Mission statements pose a different challenge. Mission and strategy often get confused. It's also common to confuse mission with objective, so let's clear this up. Mission statements capture your committed endeavor, the thing your organization is so committed to doing that they will achieve it or die trying. That's how a mission should feel. Your mission statement is the answer to, "Why the hell am I here?" The Malwarebytes mission statement is, "Our mission is to create the best disinfection and protection solutions to combat the world's most harmful Internet threats."2 That's their "committed endeavor," and they work on it every day.

Let's use the terrorism example again. What's the committed endeavor of an organization trying to rid the world of terrorism? Probably something like, "Our mission is to fight terror in all its forms anywhere in the world it poses a threat." It sounds simple, but it's an effective description of the mission. Let's take a look at JFK's stated mission for space travel, that the United States "should commit itself to achieving the goal, before this decade is out, of landing a man on the moon and returning him safely to Earth." That was the thing they were going to achieve or die trying. And people did die trying.

Mission statements reinforce existing behavior rather than guide it. A good mission statement is like a set of guardrails for your business, reminding everyone what matters. How do you figure out the right way to express your committed endeavor? Look at yourself in the mirror and ask, *Am I really willing to commit to this? Is my organization really able to achieve this? Are we willing to do what it takes to succeed?*

Mission statements are like vision statements, in that no one gives a shit about them if they're unrealistic. It's better to reduce the burden of your committed endeavor to something achievable than to live a lie.

---

2   "Malwarebytes," Glassdoor. Last modified August 31, 2020, https://www.glassdoor.com/Overview/Working-at-Malwarebytes-EI_ IE680788.11,23.htm

An impractical or uninspiring mission statement is a sure sign there's a Kabuki Dancer in charge.

We will return to vision and mission later in this chapter. Then, in the Kill Shot chapter, when you read about brand promise, you will see the importance of an accurate mission statement. By accurate, I mean one you can accomplish and one that resembles your brand promise. Think of mission like the big brother or big sister of your brand promise. If you can't see the resemblance, either your mission or your brand is off.

A mission statement–brand promise mismatch is fatal. It means there's been a deliberate attempt to scam the market into believing a promise that will never come true. Sometimes this is just incompetence, but that's being generous. And just like in every other facet of life, promise breakers eventually get found out and erased in the minds of those who were depending on them. Strategy mistakes can be fixed; I can teach you how to get yourself out of those traps. But if you can't keep your promises to the market, you are doomed. That's why you *must* pay attention to the relationship to mission and brand promise. It's *always* better to alter those for consistency than to live a lie.

We'll return to brand, mission, vision, and their relationship to value soon. Next up, how business gravity emerges in the first place.

The Inner Core and Your Target Customer

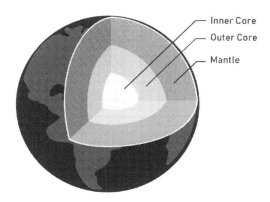

Figure 1.2 Earth's inner core, outer core, and mantle (cross section).

- **Inner core**: The value type—functional, emotional, or economic—that generates the majority of your gravity as perceived by your target customer.
- **Target customer**: The buyer whom your inner core's gravity is most likely to attract.

So, just to recap, innovation creates value, value creates mass, and mass creates gravity. Big Mass = Big Gravity. Small Mass = Small Gravity. Mass is the amount of gravity created by the three types of value emanating from your offer, where the inner core is composed of the most valuable aspect of your offer. I hope this concept is now burned into your brain. Let's focus now on your offer's primary value type, the inner core.

Look at fig. 1.2. Your inner core is that molten center. It's typically responsible for producing about 70 percent of your offer's perceived value. The second most important layer (value type) represents only about 20 percent of your offer's perceived value. The final layer represents just 10 percent.

Neglecting or misinterpreting the relationship between your inner core and your target customer is fatal. It isn't complicated, but it's amazing how often people mess it up. Your target customer is trying to buy a tool to get a job done. That job is best accomplished with a tool that is most aligned with the job.

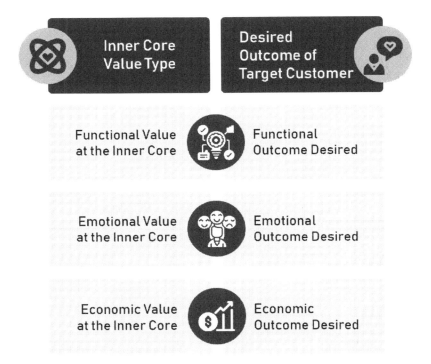

Figure 1.3 The relationship between value and outcome.

As you can see from fig. 1.3, aligning your inner core with your target customer is stupidly easy, as long as you accurately identify your inner core. So how do you do that?

How to Identify Your Inner Core

Identifying your inner core starts with identifying your "superpowers." What do I mean by superpower? It's the thing that, if taken away, makes you ordinary. Superman without his superpowers is just another dude. Adele without her voice is just another woman. Google without their algorithms would be just another search engine.

Your inner core creates the gravity that pulls customers toward your offer. Strong inner core, strong gravity; weak inner core, weak gravity. The terms *pull market* and *push market* stem from this idea. In business, strong inner cores pull customers in. Weak inner cores require that you push your offer into the marketplace. It doesn't take a rocket scientist to understand how much more valuable it is to pull customers in. Nothing is more hopeless than a company with a weak inner core run by Kabuki Dancers.

One of my favorite inner core examples comes from Jeffrey Moore, who used Tiger Woods to explain the idea. What value type is at the inner core of a professional athlete? Golf, like any sport, is a functional skill. So the inner core value type—the superpower—of Tiger Woods, the thing that would cripple him the most if taken away, is his functional ability to play golf at the highest level.

Jeff Moore talks about core versus context. Core is the thing that's unique to Tiger, and context is the resulting value produced by it. Tiger Woods produced a $500 million business selling everything from clothes to clubs to golf course architecture. And he earned about $10 million a year actually playing golf. So Moore posed the following question: Every morning when Tiger wakes up, he must choose between going to the practice range or going to the office. Which should he choose?

Playing golf produces $10 million, but running a golf empire produces $500 million. Logic would imply he should head to the office each morning and maybe hit some balls during lunch. After all, what's $10 million compared to $500 million? I'm guessing you've already figured it out. Tiger figured it out. Every morning, he wakes up and plays golf. He knows that winning golf tournaments fuels the core that created all the value of his brand.

Here's another good core example from Malwarebytes. I first heard of the company in 2008 when I was at Trend Micro. The chief information security officer (CISO) from one of our largest customers called me very pissed off. This customer had purchased our premium "Diamond" support, our highest-level service offering that included a dedicated technical account manager (TAM), whose sole responsibility was to investigate and deal with any possible virus or malware infection.

"Why the hell am I paying you two hundred thousand bucks a year for this TAM when all he does is clean our computers with this free tool called Malwarebytes?" the CISO asked me. "How about I save the two hundred grand and just use the free tool myself?"

What the hell is Malwarebytes? I kept that thought to myself. I tried to explain that our TAM service was considerably more valuable than any free tool. I also promised to look into the situation and get back to him.

I learned two things. First, my customer found the Malwarebytes free tool more valuable than my TAM. Second, Malwarebytes had built something functionally unique. We had built a pretty good virus removal tool ten years earlier called HouseCall, but we failed to keep the technology up to par against the rigors of modern malware. Other security companies fared no better. There's no way to mitigate what you can't find.

The CISO cancelled our service and left. I, too, left Trend Micro, eventually joining Malwarebytes as senior vice president (SVP) of sales. I tell you this because the Malwarebytes origin story perfectly exemplifies the power of a core with strong business gravity—it pulls.

Let's rewind a few years. Around the same time information security products started failing, a fourteen-year-old named Marcin Kleczynski was pirating video games and got his parents' PC infected with malware. So he did what any fourteen-year-old would do. He rode his bike to Borders Books, bought *Visual Basic for Dummies*, taught himself to write VB code, and developed the world's first fully automated malware removal tool.

The tech community that cares about fighting cybercrime (sometimes called "white hats") didn't hesitate to help this kid. Two such people cofounded Malwarebytes with Marcin, and several others still work at the company. In 2008, they launched the Malwarebytes tool for free. The timing couldn't have been better. Malware was exploding due to criminal hacking, existing tools weren't working, and as we all know now, the problem was only going to get worse.

The results were incredible. Malwarebytes downloads reached tens of thousands per day. The word was out, especially among computer technicians. This free tool could find and remove malware that other premium products missed. Not only was Malwarebytes helping home users, IT professionals were using it at work. Even the technicians of other security companies like Trend Micro used the free Malwarebytes tool instead of their own product. Malwarebytes went from a cult following to mainstream in both consumer and business cybersecurity. There was no question about the Malwarebytes inner core—it was the best functional tool to find and remove malware that others missed.

Without knowing how to articulate it, even fourteen-year-old Marcin understood the significance of core. He founded his company for only one purpose—being functionally superior at remediating malware. That's what makes Malwarebytes unique. That's their superpower. To this day, malware removal—called remediation—is the inner core of the Malwarebytes value stack proposition and holds together their entire strategy.

These stories probably have you wondering what your inner core is. Here's a simple test to find it. Ask yourself, *What's the one thing about my offer that, if taken away, would cripple it the most?* The answer almost always identifies your core.

While I was working at Malwarebytes, our chief marketing officer (CMO), Rebecca Kline, retained a top Silicon Valley consulting firm called Zoom Marketing to help her identify what customers value the most in a security product. Zoom refers to this as the "point that matters." The research process included a second concept that Zoom called "the hill." Basically, the hill is synonymous with the inner core. Your hill must be defended, or you risk losing everything.

I'll never forget the look on Marcin's face after Zoom presented their findings.

"Did we really just spend a hundred and thirty-five thousand dollars for someone to tell us that remediation is our hill?" I asked him on the way out of the meeting.

"I was just wondering the exact same thing," he said.

While our impulse was to tell Zoom, "Thank you, Captain Obvious," we knew better.

Because finding your inner core is worth it. Even when it seems obvious. You cannot successfully build your Moonshot if you get your inner core wrong.

And sometimes your core is just *not* that obvious. Then what do you do? Ask yourself, *What's our secret sauce? What are our superpowers? Why are our customers willing to bet on us?* Your business exists for a purpose, and there's something unique about the value it creates.

Still can't find the answer? Go back to that first question, but let's broaden it. *What's the one thing that, if taken away, would cripple this business the most?* Ninety-nine times out of a hundred, the answer will reveal your inner core.

The harsh reality is that not all inner cores are created equal. If your offer isn't resonating in the marketplace, it's probably not because you misidentified your inner core. In all likelihood, it's because the value emanating from your inner core is smaller than you realized, or it's not aligned with marketplace realities. It's not hopeless if your inner core value is small. You can always attempt to add more mass or manipulate gravity to give yourself a better chance at reaching your target customers. But don't delude yourself. Having low gravity because your inner core is weak is brutally hard to overcome.

You cannot pivot your inner core unless you're willing to start from scratch. Michael Jordan couldn't pivot to baseball, and Mick Jagger couldn't pivot to acting (watch *Performance* if you don't believe me). Their actual inner cores gave Jordan and Jagger platforms to try new things, but they sucked at them, so no new legitimate cores were created, and therefore little value creation resulted. You can pivot every other aspect of the Moonshot, but you can't pivot your inner core unless you're willing to start from scratch. Core is discrete. It must stand on its own. As a business gets big, it can add more value by creating additional Moonshots, but at the center of every Moonshot must be a core.

Value Types

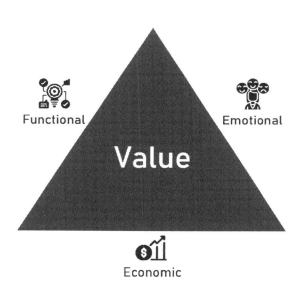

Figure 1.4 The Value Triangle.

To create a successful Moonshot and become a Shot Caller, you must understand how humans perceive value—and how to manipulate those perceptions. Here's the deal. The Value Triangle you see in fig. 1.4 is the totality of how humans perceive value. That's true 100 percent of the time for 100 percent of purchases. This never changes. All value from now until the end of time will be perceived as a combination of these three value types anytime value is exchanged. Maybe some alien species somewhere sees value differently, but I highly doubt it.

You will always stack all three every time you put your offer on the market. Again, 70 percent of perceived value is contained in the inner core, 20 percent in the outer core, and 10 percent in the mantle. These percentages are not exact and there is no exact data on them, but this is close. It's based on everything I could find on the subject and my own experience and experimentation. Therefore, use your judgement when you think about your value stack. Some offers are almost entirely perceived as the value of the inner core, while others are perceived more equally. My starting point is always 70-20-10 unless I learn otherwise.

Remember, your task is to identify the value type emanating from the inner core of your offer, and it's almost always functional or emotional. Economic value is only at the inner core of an offer that is a pure commodity. So if you think your inner core emits economic value, send me an email, and I'll show you the way.

The Three *R*s: Rationalize, Resolve, Reaffirm

There is one more reality about giving humans what they want and expect when it comes to value. I call it the Three *R*s: **Rationalize, Resolve, Reaffirm**. Have you ever tested your offer to see if it has achieved "product-market fit"? That's when the buyer is able to **rationalize** your functional value, **resolve** their emotional need to feel either superior or satisfied, and have their perception of economic value **reaffirmed** through the buying process. I say reaffirm rather than affirm because perception is never ending. Every time you perceive value, you are questioning its worthiness, especially once the allure of the shiny new object wears off. Just ask anyone who bought a Louis Vuitton how they feel about their purchase one year later.

One final point here. We all know the expression "bang for the buck," which refers to the idea of how much we perceived that an exchange of value was worth it. Pay attention to the relationship between that phrase and the Three *R*s Test. Here's the shortcut:

- Anytime your inner core is based on functional or emotional superiority value, your customer is looking for the "bang." They are seeking superior performance and are buying your offer <u>despite</u> its price.
- Anytime your inner core is based on emotional satisfaction, your customer is looking for "bang for the buck." They are seeking good enough performance and are buying your offer <u>because</u> of the price.

Rationalize Functional Value

Let's talk about the inner core that contains functional value. Some easy examples of offers where the inner core is likely to be functional include the cloud, cybersecurity, computer networking, sales productivity tools, and sports cars. Any industry where buyers demand high performance is likely to be on a functional inner core. Remember, these customers are looking for "bang" and need to be convinced of your product's functional advantage. Functional value must be rationalized using objective criteria. Your target buyer must rationalize your value. Feed them data, stats, performance metrics, etc., but make sure it's as objectively measurable as possible.

Resolve Emotional Value

Your target customers are going to have all kinds of emotions running through them, but there are only two emotions you need to account for when it comes to emotional value—superiority or satisfaction. It will always be one or the other, never both. That's not to say that an offer that only aims to satisfy can't also make the customer feel superior, but that's not how to think about emotional value. You must resolve for the target emotional outcome. If you end up exceeding expectations, meaning your offer was intended to be good enough but made the customer feel more than satisfied, there is a high risk that you are overserving the market. That's not necessarily a bad outcome, as long as that's what your economic strategy called for. In any case, the good news is, resolving these emotions is simple when you know your inner core.

Emotional value must be demonstrated with subjective criteria. Either make sure your customer feels superior or feels satisfied with the outcome of your offer. Let's discuss these two emotions.

Superiority

I refer to this as the "more is more" emotion. Humans expect to feel like they've made the superior choice when buying offers that are supposed to deliver "the bang." Some examples of offers where the inner core is likely to be based on emotional superiority are luxury goods, high-end experiences and entertainment, cosmetic surgery, private jet service, and other offers where the buyer wants first and foremost to *feel* superior.

Be careful; it's easy to confuse functional value with "more is more" emotional value. Customers who buy based on a functional inner core put functionality first. *Then* they want to feel superior. But it's the opposite if the inner core is based on emotional value. In that case, your value stack leads with emotional value and reinforces with functional value as the outer core. Someone demanding to feel superior won't be happy with just being satisfied.

Satisfaction

I refer to this as the "less is more" or "good enough is good enough" emotion. This is the buyer who is looking for a lot of "bang for their buck." If your product or service offers an economic benefit (e.g., better deal, best price, etc.), humans are usually OK with being underserved. A great example is what the Japanese did to the American auto industry with the introduction of less expensive, reliable, "good enough" cars.

Detroit watched the wolf walk right up to their door and did nothing until it was too late.

Another emotional satisfaction example is Salesforce.com. They started by selling easy-to-use "software as a service" (SaaS) to SMB customers. Their phone number was something like 800-No-Software. They offered a customer relationship management (CRM) tool that was good enough and didn't attempt to overserve the market with complex features. Instead, they focused on customers who valued a good enough tool at an attractive cost. (Eventually, both Japanese automakers and Salesforce.com eventually went upmarket, creating offers that went from good enough to superior.).

It's critically important to grasp that a customer's perception of value changes over time. They may start off feeling that "less is more," but over time will decide to pay for the added value of a superior offer. Conversely, they may start off needing to feel superior, but as time goes on, they realize they're just fine feeling satisfied with the economic benefit.

You must recognize this distinct shift because your business must shift as well. This classic "innovator's dilemma" occurs when businesses feel the need to perpetually overserve or underserve their customers even after the customers' perception of value has changed, forcing themselves out of orbit. This opens the door for opposing gravity (your competitors) to fill the gap.

Reaffirm Economic Value

In very few instances is economic value perceived as the inner core. It happens when an offer is a commodity like gas or water, but even those can be perceived for their functional or emotional value. We've all spent five dollars on a fancy bottle of water packaged to make us feel superior. How I rejoice at the sight of losers sucking from a water fountain as I gracefully sip my bottle of Fuji Water. Or is it Fiji? Who cares? I have it, and you don't!

Economic value is probably not your inner core. Instead, think of economic value as a compensating mechanism to get and remain in orbit with your customers. You are compensating for deficits in functional or emotional value. I always ask the buyer, "How are you feeling?" I am seeking to determine if I have successfully rationalized functional value and made them feel superior or satisfied, depending on what my objective was. Economic value is typically used to bring the first two value elements into balance. It's that win-win scenario when the exchange of value is worth it for both the buyer and the seller—unless you're trying to disrupt or dominate the market. Then economic value does *not* seek balance. It's *not* intended to get your customer into orbit. It's intended to add more mass to your offer. That's usually achieved through discounting, and it works. The problem is that adding mass by reducing price isn't sustainable, so you must use this strategy wisely, i.e., sparingly.

Economic value can also be reaffirmed by reinforcing what the customer wants to believe. This is the "make peace" part of the buying process. Your customer wants to reconcile their decision and feel good about the value of your offer. We all know what it's like to feel buyer's remorse, that feeling that something wasn't worth it. Your job here is to create the opposite effect. A simple phone call to a new customer is a good example of reinforcement.

Value Stacking

Value stacking is the process of layering how you intend to have customers perceive you in the market. The most important layer of your offer's value is the inner core. It sets the foundation for your value stack, which you then use to create your overall business strategy and brand promise. Step one of value stacking is to identify your inner core. From there, value stacking is the simple process of identifying your outer core and mantle. Use this grid to complete the process.

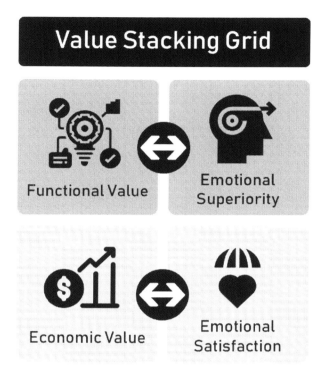

Figure 1.5 The Value Stacking Grid.

1. Identify your inner core value type based on your superpower.

2. Move horizontally on the grid to identify your outer core value type.

3. Add the remaining element to complete your value stack (remember to use only one emotional element).

4. As an exercise, try to create the value stack for your current offer.

    a. Inner Core:
    b. Outer Core:
    c. Mantle:

Just for fun, I've listed the value stacks for the last five companies I've worked at:

- **Trend Micro**: Functional, Emotional Superiority, Economic
- **ZScaler**: Functional, Emotional Superiority, Economic
- **Malwarebytes**: Functional, Emotional Superiority, Economic
- **Virsec**: Functional, Emotional Superiority, Economic
- **Emailage**: Functional, Emotional Superiority, Economic

Yes, it's boring because they're all the same. That's because my entire career has been in tech, and tech almost always has a functional inner core at the center of its mass.

Value Traps

You know what peril I've experienced over and over that screws up so many companies? Value traps. Value traps occur when company leaders don't understand (or refuse to admit) the reality of their offer's inner core value. Value traps are one of my favorite topics. They expose the fact that most people in jobs that require them to understand gravity don't. They're just Kabuki Dancers. Fortunately, these perils are easy to spot and avoid—if you know what to look for.

Size Matters

Ninety percent of all new product innovations fail because the inner core just ain't that cool. Small inner core, small value, small mass, small gravity. The most obvious advice is don't build small-inner-core shitty offers! Unfortunately, it happens all the time because innovation is hard and Kabuki Dancers love to push the "fake it till you make it" myth rather than face reality.

This trap does a ton of damage because executives often refuse to believe that their baby isn't beautiful. This leads to the next mistake—

overrelying on proximity. Here's the way out. If the mass is too small, add more. Don't overinvest in proximity. Spending a lot of money to reveal an offer with low mass to the market doesn't make it better.

Grid Jumping

The ultimate expression of Kabuki dancing is grid jumping. It's when you so deeply misunderstand your value stack that you try to be everything to everyone. You show up in the market throwing every claim of value against the wall like so much spaghetti to see what sticks. It's like playing roulette by placing a chip on every number and assuming this means you can't lose. Sure, you can't lose, but you can't win either. You don't get paid to break even; you get paid to win.

There are so many examples of grid jumping to choose from, but my favorite is from PC Matic. In one sixty-second commercial, this cybersecurity company touts functional, emotional, and economic value in at least a dozen different ways. It's for businesses and consumers and governments, it stops ransomware and phishing, it has whitelisting, it's low cost because "security isn't only for the wealthy," it's empowering, and it's made in America! And by the way, we're hiring!

Here's my simple prescription. Don't grid jump! Stack your value, putting most of your energy into the inner core, then the outer core, then the mantle.

The Chipping Away Fallacy

I once visited an Italian museum that housed some of Michelangelo's greatest sculptures. His works were truly awe inspiring. But not all of them. Some he never finished. At least, that's what I thought until the tour guide corrected me. She explained that there was no such thing as an unfinished Michelangelo. His vision wasn't to sculpt the marble. Rather, in his mind, he "released the masterpiece" from inside the marble. So-called "finished" works contained masterpieces inside; he simply released the marble confining them. Michelangelo's works that look unfinished were merely his acceptance of the reality that the marble contained no masterpiece. Some of them were just rocks at the inner core.

I've seen budgets wasted and careers ruined by chipping away at a rock that contains no masterpiece. This happens when there's a belief that if you just keep hammering away at the market, customers will eventually reward you. Think of your inner core as the center of your block of marble. Is there a masterpiece inside worth endlessly chipping away at to find? Or is it better to realize, as Michelangelo did, that the futility of chipping away at a weak inner core is a waste of time? For Shot Callers, the answer is obvious. Don't waste your time driving everyone crazy chipping away at a core that isn't very powerful.

Here's the prescription. Build a better inner core or lower your expectations until your current inner core is ready. And invest in antigravity strategies, which most companies underutilize. Chipping away using proximity investments might be futile, but adding intense antigravity strategy sometimes gets the job done.

Conditions Are Everything

I'm guessing "timing is everything" is the oldest expression in business. I can see two cave dwellers sitting around bemoaning the fact they were late investing in the wheel. But is it just timing? Or is it more complicated than that? The reality is that timing is just part of a bigger picture that's driving how likely you are to realize the value of your offer in the marketplace. For fun, ask a friend to name the three greatest generals in history. I promise you you'll get answers like Patton, Eisenhower, Washington, Napoleon, Grant, etc. Then ask, "What do they all have in common?" I promise you'll get answers like "they were all bold" or "they were all men" or "they were all strong leaders."

What you won't get is the most obvious answer of them all. There was a war when they happened to be generals! The conditions for their value to be rewarded existed on their watch. There is no way these generals were all the greatest, they were all just in the job when war broke out. Conditions created their greatness, and without those conditions, all of them would have been swept into the dustbin of history like every other general you've never heard of.

In my case, I experienced the agony (and eventually the ecstasy) of this value trap when I was with the cybersecurity company ZScaler. I spent a little over a year there in 2012 and endured a 100 percent turnover of the sales team I was running—and I was fired. We simply couldn't get the team productive, even though the founder, Jay Chaudhry, had built the most powerful "security as a service" cloud on the planet. They solved problems that were so hard to solve that the functional inner core was massive. As amazing it was, the company wasn't growing very fast.

The problem? Conditions. Jay knew how valuable the company was because he was offered a billion dollars for it before it reached $20 million in sales. But no amount of money could solve the problem of the right conditions not being in place. I asked Jay one day, "What's the most surprising thing about ZScaler?"

He answered, "How long it's taking."

Eventually, the conditions Jay was depending on to drive his Moonshot (businesses moving to the cloud and a much more dangerous cyber threat landscape) came to the forefront. ZScaler's value became easier to unlock, and they were rewarded with higher growth rates. The company announced their intention to go public in 2017 when I started writing this book. Hey, books take a long time to write!

ZScaler now has a $15 billion market cap, and I got pretty damn rich. The truth is, a lot of people made a lot of money thanks to the unwavering drive of Jay. Due to the reality of how their value was timed to the conditions of the marketplace, that success was unfortunately built on a hell of a lot of fired sales and marketing people, including me. I was pissed for a while, but I got over it. Looking back, it's clear they were simply committed to their core, and they were going to keep making changes until the right conditions existed and its value was unlocked.

Value Mis-stacking

Companies get caught in this trap when they misinterpret the market, their inner core, or their target customer. Fortunately, the value stacking grid solves for this trap, but you still have to be diligent about sticking to the stack. Now that you know your value stack has three layers, think of it like a pizza. Your inner core is the dough. Your second and third elements are the toppings. Value mis-stacking occurs when you put the toppings first and the dough second or third. That's a stupid-looking pizza. Who puts the dough *on top of* the sauce and cheese?

This trap creates confusion in the market. Perhaps you've heard the term that an offer seems like it's going "off-brand?" That's the effect created by mis-stacking. The value stack doesn't match the market's expectations. Apple does a great job of knowing their inner core and their target customer and staying "on-brand." One message stacks functional value first for their geeky customers, and another different message stacks emotional superiority value first for their status buyers. Make your pizza, add your toppings, and stick to the stack.

The next time you watch TV, look for mis-stacking in the commercials. You'll never look at advertising the same way again. It's actually fun to spot mis-stacking. With apologies to my friends at Google, their 2019 NCAA Division I Men's Basketball Tournament "March Madness" ads mis-stacked their Google Cloud offer. Done right, these commercials would have promoted Google's functional superiority in analytics compared to other cloud providers like Amazon Web Services, Microsoft, and IBM. Instead, Google reached for a far too emotional message that confuses me to this day. Instead of leaving viewers amazed by their technical superiority, they left users feeling emotionally underwhelmed. Big mistake.

Here's the prescription to avoid Google's glaring error. Be bold! Know your target customer, and lead with your inner core. And don't water it down. Correct value stacking means your primary value feels like a punch in the face. Customers want shortcuts, not mis-stacked messages that force them to figure out what the hell your primary value even is. And above all, once you nail down your value stack, stick to the stack!

The Four Strategy Moves

I'm rather certain that the following statement is the most controversial one in this book.

There are only four strategies available to all businesses, and each must be accounted for.

I've been a student of strategy most of my business life. I've revered the great strategy thinkers. I've built upon everything these giants have taught. But I knew something was off. Creating strategy always seemed mysterious, complicated, and hard. So I fixed it. Now, what exactly is strategy?

Strategy is altering gravity to maximize your chance of achieving your objective.

Remember reading this definition in the intro heading? It probably didn't make sense then, but by now it should. Get comfortable with this definition of strategy. Because it works. I've led the strategy creation exercises for Trend Micro's enterprise business, for Malwarebytes, for Virsec, and for Emailage. The strategies we developed and employed didn't make money fall from the sky, and they didn't miraculously create value. After all, innovation creates value. But those strategies did what *all* strategies are supposed to do—maximize the chance of winning! Do I deserve the credit for winning? No! Do I deserve the credit for leading the strategy creation? Yes! Can you win without the right strategy? No! Connect the dots any way you want. I've never cared who created the winning strategy. I only cared that we *had* a winning strategy.

How many winning strategies for significant companies have you created? I'm guessing zero. And why is that? Because this task is assigned to the founders, investors, consultants, and the C-level executive team. Who else besides these geniuses could possibly figure this shit out? You, that's who! We've all been so sold on how hard and complicated strategy is that we just assume that only the top dogs can do it. Well, that bullshit stops right now. Anyone—that means you—can create a world-class strategy if you keep reading and buy in to Shot Calling.

One note before we get into the four strategy moves. The strategic decision to maximize your chances of winning must be made by *you*. I'm giving you the easiest possible way to avoid common mistakes. But *you* must make the decision. And once you understand the four strategy moves, it's not hard to create a winning strategy.

You will use the Whole Shot Grid to design your Whole Shot Grid (the fourth and final deliverable of your Moonshot). Remember, you're altering gravity to maximize your chances of achieving your objective. You've learned about value types (functional, emotional, economic) and you've learned about gravity levers (mass, proximity, opposing gravity, super gravity). You've also learned how you can compensate for deficits in gravity using the Three *R*s Test. Now it's time to put it all together. This is what we've been working toward, the relationship between value and strategy. This where you also have to state your key performance indicators (KPIs) or OKRs (objective and key results). Master these, and you will become a Shot Caller capable of contributing at the highest level of any company.

You should know your value stack by now, and your target customer must be aligned to your inner core. For example, don't target a highly differentiated functional inner core at a customer who simply wants emotional satisfaction.

Set your objective and time frame. Your strategy will typically target a revenue objective, and I strongly recommend doing so unless you're using "zero barrier, delayed reward" super gravity (more on that soon). In that case, your objective may be something like user count, market share, or some other nonrevenue measurement. But use revenue whenever you can because that's the best scorecard in business. Also, any decent strategy should last for at least three years, so set your time frame to three years to achieve your objective unless you have a reason to make it longer or shorter.

I've been asked a million times if there's a formula for calculating gravity. Sure, in nature there is, but for our purposes, we're not going to try to calculate gravity, mass, or opposing gravity. Use the tools I've given you to assess how much gravity you create or how much opposing gravity you face. You can get pretty good data through Outcome-Driven Innovation techniques, which you can read about in *What Customers Want*. I highly recommend this approach.

Let's go over each strategy move.

Strategy Move 1: Mass

Remember, your goal is to alter gravity to maximize your chances of achieving your objective. And since value is always perceived in three ways (functional, emotional, economic) the question for each strategy move becomes *What can I alter functionally, emotionally, or economically to improve my chances of success?*

Here are some suggestions for mass, but don't limit your ideas to just these.

- Functional Mass: Add features, capabilities, performance, and anything else that can be measured objectively.
- Emotional Mass: Add reporting, design, flow, feel, pedigree, heritage, and anything else that can be assessed subjectively.
- Economic Mass: Decide if you intend to appropriately serve the market or if you want to unbalance economic gravity by over- or underserving your customer (I'll explain this in Strategy Move 3).

What? How the hell am I supposed to know how to amplify the value of my inner core? I'm not an engineer! I'm not an executive!

Trust me, most engineers and executives don't have a clue how to do this! The obvious answer is almost always the best answer. Let me tell you what I did at Trend Micro to add more mass to the core.

As GM of enterprise business, it was my responsibility to set the strategy for winning large customers. I hired the Chasm Group consulting company, and we spent three months and around $125,000 searching for our "sustainable competitive advantage." A worthy effort. We examined eighteen different options. I don't remember them all, but we hammered away at them, testing and validating to come up with a short list.

Then one day, it hit me. This thing called the "cloud" was a technology that all the engineers were talking about as the best way to process and distribute cyber threat protection. The coolest part was that our customers could participate in improving their own results because cloud technology was capable of automatically learning about cyber threats. We could use that knowledge to help our other customers. Today, we call this a network effect, and it's an awesome way to add value without adding more resources (and it's a great example of a super gravity strategy at work). But in 2008, it had no name, at least not in the cybersecurity industry. So when I called my CEO to pitch it, I jokingly suggested we should call it "social security." She laughed at the joke, but not the idea. We agreed immediately that *that* was our core, eliminated all the other short-list strategies, and put all of our focus on bringing the cloud to the cybersecurity market. Nine months later, we launched Smart Protection as our central pillar of value. As of this writing, it's still at the core of Trend Micro's value stack proposition.

The next big move I accomplished was acquiring the company Third Brigade. Their technology protected cloud workloads wherever they ran. Don't worry if you don't know what that means, it doesn't matter. The point is that the acquisition added tremendous mass to our core because it allowed us to tell our target customer that we had "security *from* the cloud" and "security *for* the cloud." A ton of people had to approve, build, and execute this strategy, but it all started with creating the strategy first. It worked, by the way. Trend Micro is considered number one in cloud security. The insignificant little acquisition now accounts for a large part of Trend Micro's overall value.

That's the ultimate test for a Shot Caller. *Did I call the shot, and was I right?* Success has a thousand fathers, but failure is an orphan. As sure as God made little green apples, you *will* be blamed if you call your shot and miss, so be sure to accrue your successes to your personal brand.

Add mass to your own personal core as you add mass to a business core. That's what builds careers and helps you on your journey toward becoming an executive.

Strategy Move 2: Proximity

Proximity isn't just about showing up, it's about *how* you show up. Once your offer has sufficient mass, your next move is to get as close to your target customers as necessary to achieve your objective. Notice I didn't say "get as close to customers as possible." That's overkill. The key is to understand which emotional state you want your target customer to feel (superiority or satisfaction) and get close enough to them to create the desired effect. The tools at your disposal to affect your proximity are:

- Human to human: any form of human outreach to directly engage the customer (e.g., an outside salesperson meeting prospects at a trade show booth)
- Machine to human: any form of digital outreach to indirectly engage the customer (e.g., digital advertising to promote a free software trial)
- Brand to human: any form of content to influence the customer (e.g., the company blog, newsletter, and social media posts)

Strategy Move 3: Antigravity

The most common form of antigravity is some kind of discount for your offer. I've built and run deal desks (a team that reviews pricing) for the last fifteen years. You might as well call them antigravity desks. That's because in some way the customer is saying, "Your offer just doesn't have enough mass to compel me to buy it." So you lower the price. There's nothing wrong with that, but don't be a Kabuki Dancer and use discounting as a crutch.

Remember when I mentioned the book *What Customers Want?* Read it. The premise is simple—**products are tools to help customers get jobs done**. This line has guided my thoughts on business for the last dozen years, and it will continue to do so until something better replaces it. The reason it's so compelling is that everyone in business faces the same question. *What the hell do my customers really value?* So read this book to find the answer.

This book also helped me realize that knowing what customers want isn't enough. Some other force is at play. A force that seems to hold your target customer in place. That force is the opposing gravity you've been reading about, and it's not created equal among all offers. Sometimes it's intensely strong; other times much less so. I don't have an exact formula (at least not yet), but you can estimate the force of opposing gravity (AKA competitors' pull) using the Opposing Gravity Grid (fig. 1.1). It's a good way to understand what you're up against as you bring your offer to market. I can't tell you how many times winning was way harder than anyone thought it would be. And sure, there are some elements of winning you *can* control, like becoming a Shot Caller.

The best antigravity strategies weaken competitors' gravity by starting with their primary value type and targeting their inner core.

We used my favorite antigravity strategy at Malwarebytes. We mined data from the cloud and displayed the failure rates of competing products. Here's how it worked. Every day, tens of thousands of computer users would let Malwarebytes scan their machines looking for malware infections. And every day we found thousands of infected computers. Our data science team was able to track which particular form and version of malware was infecting each computer. They were also able to determine which security product those computers had been using. Nearly every time we found malware, we also found out which security product had failed to protect that computer.

Our data science team also created a way to easily visualize the failure of these competing products. I could literally ask a prospect, "What security product are you using?" and show them the exact malware we were detecting on machines protected by that very product. The other product was literally failing right before their eyes! You should have seen the pissed off look on their faces!

The bar is high when your value stack is functional at the inner core. Functional inner cores must produce the feeling of superiority. People get pissed when they don't get it, especially if they paid a premium price for the product. A unit of antigravity is just as powerful as a unit of gravity. But antigravity can sometimes be far more efficient than gravity, so at some level it can even be more powerful than altering mass or proximity. Do not overlook this strategy!

Strategy Move 4: Super Gravity

One of my favorite TV shows is *How the Universe Works*. The truth is, no one has a clue how the universe works, but we know a lot more than we used to. We have a good idea how stars form. Gravity gets the ball rolling, heat and immense pressure do the rest, and shazam! Atomic fusion creates a star. The best part is that fusion creates more energy than it consumes, creating immense amounts of free energy to harvest. Scientists have been trying to recreate fusion on this planet for decades but have yet to succeed.

The good news is that fusion is possible in business when you get more value out than you put in. This can create massive new gravity, so I call this super gravity. Simply put, the definition for super gravity is **any strategy that improves mass or proximity disproportionately to the resource expended**. These are the $1 + 1 = 3$ strategies that create more value, growth, and profits than the other three strategies because they produce exponential outcomes. (You can check out Metcalfe's law to understand this better.)

We executed super gravity strategies at both Malwarebytes and Emailage. Malwarebytes gave away free malware remediation software to gain market awareness and, more importantly, to make the marketplace feel that their technology was superior. Emailage convinced customers to share instances of online fraud detections in order to make the service better for every customer using it. The strength of the founders for both of these companies was their capacity to recognize these opportunities and seize upon them.

There are only three categories of super gravity to examine. They largely align with the three forms of value you learned about.

1. **Network effect** aligns primarily to functional value. It occurs when adding more users automatically adds more functional mass to the offer. Facebook is a famous example. Every time Facebook adds a new user, every other subscriber receives the benefit of that person's network. Pretty much any strategy for a social platform is betting on the network effect form of super gravity.

   At Emailage, our form of network effect was outsmarting fraud together. That's literally the brand promise. What it means is each time an Emailage customer shares information about an online fraud incident, that information helps stop fraud for other customers.

2. **Zero barrier, delayed reward** aligns primarily to emotional value. This form of super gravity is all about removing barriers for people to use your offer while delaying the rewards your company earns from having them use your offer. Open-source software like Linux and Android are great examples. Linux companies make money offering professional tech support services to Linux programmers. In Google's case, the Android open-source operating system supports Google's primary revenue stream, advertising. Open-source Android means Android phones cost less to manufacture. Cheaper phones, more customers. More phone users, more advertising opportunities. Zero barriers, big rewards.

   My favorite story about this type of super gravity strategy is Malwarebytes. I'm certain fourteen-year-old Marcin Kleczynski had no idea how big his idea would become. I'm also quite certain he didn't consciously create a "super gravity strategy" when he decided to let people use his technology for free. He was just pissed at the assholes spreading malware. Y*ou didn't pay to get infected, you shouldn't pay to get disinfected* was his philosophy. So he made his software available for free, and the use of it took off like a rocket ship. By now, this software has been downloaded billions of times. Millions and millions of people use it every year, and it finds billions of malware infections. And the infected computers almost always have some other cybersecurity product installed.

It doesn't take a genius to figure out that if you're using a computer protected by a product that failed, then the product that found and removed the failure is *superior*. I often wore Malwarebytes shirts when I traveled. I was frequently stopped and thanked by people who had their asses saved by this software. A security guard brought me to the front of the check-in line at a hotel once he saw my shirt. A TSA screener pulled me out of line to thank me. Random people tapping me on the shoulder just to say thank you was a common occurrence.

At Malwarebytes, this form of super gravity was my favorite strategy move because it didn't require a ton of resources, it made people feel superior, it generated tremendous goodwill for the brand, and it drove the sales of the paid products to over $150 million a year. That's the power of this strategy.

3. **Value chain** aligns to economic value. When done well, it can also create a lot of opposing gravity for your competitors to deal with. It occurs when companies prearrange the reward system for each other every time value is exchanged. Microsoft developer strategy, Salesforce AppExchange, Amazon Prime, eBay, Visa, Uber—there are many examples of companies working together to create value chains. I've spent most of my career participating in value chains, largely through distribution channels that extend the reach and expertise of our own sales efforts.

However, don't mistake "building your channel" for this form of super gravity. You must get more out than you put in for this strategy to qualify as super gravity. In cybersecurity, Symantec deserves the most credit for succeeding here. They executed a strategy to "dominate at the point of distribution," and it worked, at least for a while. Then they entirely screwed up their company with the insane decision to merge with Veritas. That's another story.

One final note on super gravity. You can use more than one type. Take Facebook. They started with zero barrier, delayed reward in combination with the network effect. Once they started monetizing through ads, they added the value chain. No wonder governments all over the world want to break them up.

Same with Google. Their search engine is free (zero barrier, delayed reward), the search results improve for all participants the more their service is used (network effect), and they have the most profitable value chain ever built with their ecosystem of media companies and other third parties, producing over $1 trillion in shareholder value. And just like Facebook, governments around the world are suing them.

And in case you're wondering, super gravity can create immense opposing gravity. Just ask anyone who has ever tried to take on Google or Facebook.

It's also important to understand that not all offers can benefit from super gravity. Sometimes, the conditions for super gravity to occur simply aren't there. But if they are, go for it. While there's risk, there is also massive potential.

Gravity Shifting

Now that you've learned about mass, proximity, antigravity, and super gravity, what if your strategies are not good enough? What if these alone are not creating the outcomes necessary to reach your objectives?

Remember, your customer must be able to **rationalize** your functional value, **resolve** their emotional need to feel either superior or satisfied, and have their perception of economic value **reaffirmed** through the entire buying process. This is the Three *R*s Test we talked about earlier. It plays no favorites. Something is off if you are not winning, and it doesn't necessarily require a complete strategy overhaul to fix. You just need to make adjustments to shift gravity enough to win.

Discounting is the easiest gravity shift there is. It happens all the time. But if you simply put your offer on sale, or you discount your offer just because the customer wants to save money, you're not discounting correctly. Save discounting strategies for instances when customers are captive to opposing gravity or when winning the customer is more important than preserving margins.

Here are a few examples of how I shifted gravity without making big strategy or pricing changes. At Trend Micro, we faced a classic problem: a deadly combination of increased competitive pressure and diminishing technical superiority. On top of that, our packaging was extremely granular. At one point, we had over fifteen thousand combinations of products and pricing possibilities. Customers took advantage of this packaging by buying only what they needed, and our average sales price plummeted. Our gravity shift was to create product bundles. We completely overhauled our packaging. Combining the most essential technologies together gave us the best chance to create maximum perception of value. This shift worked well, and our average selling price (ASP) more than doubled within twenty-four months.

At Emailage, we faced the opposite problem. The entire service was packaged into a simple price and transaction approach. It was impossible for the customer's perception of value to lean in our favor. The gravity shift here was achieved through decoupling. Elements of our offer that were not priced individually (services, consulting, reporting tools) were given a price, forcing the customer to perceive their value. This shift is projected to increase the average sale by a minimum of 35 percent.

In both cases, the gravity shift didn't require anything but marketing resources to make the strategy successful. Sometimes, small tweaks to mass, proximity, or antigravity do the trick. Other times, conditions may not be right for your offer and it's best to rethink which target customers make the most sense to pursue. It's also imperative to evaluate your mission statement during these times of adjustment. There is no way you are going to win if your mission isn't realistic. It's far better to reduce your mission parameters than delude yourself into believing you are setting yourself up to win with an aggressive mission statement. You're not. You're setting yourself up for failure, so steer clear of doomed missions. Seems obvious, but this happens all the time.

Strategy Traps

In *Dealing with Darwin*, Geoffrey Moore writes that the mistake most people make with strategy isn't that they go too far, it's that they don't go far enough. I've seen this almost everywhere I've ever been, and you probably have too. I believe it's because there simply aren't enough Shot Callers in business. Shot Callers have a better understanding of what it takes to win; therefore, they have a better understanding of the perils they face. This makes them much freer to pursue bold strategies rather than play it safe. More on this in the Three-Point Shot.

Fear-based Kabuki Dancer leaders are a big part of the problem that causes strategy choices to be weak and timid. Just as there are four strategy moves, there's a trap for each of them. To avoid peril, you must avoid these traps. Some will seem obvious, others not so much. Here they are, with my experiences as examples. Some of these stories still piss me off.

Mass out the Ass

Imagine being locked in a building with teams of engineers, marketers, executives, product managers, and Kabuki Dancers working on creating something with as much mass as possible. You want it to have mass out the ass before you reveal your offer to the world. You all toil away, and finally it's ready. You probably congratulate one another on your genius, convinced that your "baby" is beautiful. I'm guilty of those thoughts as I sit here writing this. *Damn, this gravity shit is pure genius!* It's human nature to believe in the value of what we create, but it doesn't matter what we think. It only matters what the market thinks.

The movie *He's Just Not That Into You* is a perfect metaphor for this mass strategy trap. The characters in the film torture themselves trying to figure out if they're liked by the person they like. As the title implies, they don't always get the answer they want. Their offer (themselves) has low mass and subsequently low gravity attracting their target customer (the person they want to be with). The next move would be to affect proximity—call the other person, kiss the other person, etc. But what if the other person doesn't respond? What if the other person isn't buying what you're selling? What if the other person "just isn't that into you"? It's a failure, and more often than not it's a painful one.

The same thing happens in business all the time. An offer doesn't have enough mass, but you bring it to market anyway. You desperately create proximity strategies, but sales are poor. The Kabuki Dancers start dropping lines like "fake it till you make it" and make idiotic references to Steve Jobs's advice that you need to "create a reality distortion field." What bullshit. The truth is, the mass is too small to create enough gravity, especially if opposing gravity is intense.

Then what? What's the right thing to do? It's simple. Don't execute on proximity strategies that the market isn't going to reward! I've never seen investments in proximity pay off if the mass is too low.

The only exception is when opposing gravity is weak. Use the Opposing Gravity Grid to make this determination. If you do indeed have a new tool to address a new job, you have the opportunity to be a first mover. That can create a huge advantage, so be bold and go for it. Conversely, if you're bringing a new tool to get an old job done, opposing gravity is going to be intense, and low mass is never going to move the needle. Use the Opposing Gravity Grid. Don't be a Kabuki Dancer and ignore it, because you will be a victim of this trap if you do.

The best (or worst, really) example of this that I experienced was at Trend Micro with a product called InterScan Gateway Security Appliance (IGSA). It was designed to stop viruses at the gateway. Don't worry if you don't know what this means. The important thing to know is that it was overpriced with inferior function. It did not have mass out the ass.

This product also faced intense opposing gravity. Its value stack was functional at the inner core, but in no way did it make a customer feel superior because it wasn't. I wish we would've had the Opposing Gravity Grid back then.

The inside sales VP at Trend Micro, Vince Kearns, and his team in Dallas led the sales push for this product. They did a great job creating proximity. They designed an incentive program for the product and cleverly referred to IGSA as "I Gotta Sell Another." Unfortunately, the market had other ideas. Turns out it's tough to sell low-mass products locked in place by intense opposing gravity. Who knew? You do now, so don't fall into this trap.

The prescription here is to be honest. It's not the low mass that gets companies killed, it's the belief that there's more mass than there is, or that opposing gravity is some kind of hoax dreamed up by the sales and marketing teams.

The right choice is to be a Shot Caller. Use these tools to create a strategy with an objective that's attainable and then alter gravity as effectively as possible. I promise you will get better results than some heroic "once more unto the breach" attempt to win by brute force. More importantly, you and your co-workers will develop your Shot-Calling muscles.

Close Only Counts in Horseshoes and Hand Grenades

Proximity is about being totally committed to helping customers rationalize functional value, resolve emotional value, and reaffirm economic value. That leads us to the biggest proximity trap of all: close only counts in horseshoes and hand grenades.

Remember, your inner and outer core represent about 90 percent of the perceived value of your offer. Be honest. Are you and your company committed to unlocking this value? Most of the time, the answer is "mostly" or "kinda." But close enough isn't good enough, because someone will come along and fully commit to serving your customer better than you. They will burn the boats and, in the process, they'll burn your ass.

In 2002, Trend Micro had reached $330 million in revenue but had stopped growing. A fairly common story. Good initial mass, good gravity, low opposing gravity, decent proximity moves, customers seemingly happy and orbiting well. So why did the growth stop? Because growth always stops when your gravity is no longer strong enough.

To their credit, the CEO and family (Steve, Eva, Jenny) hired Accenture to explore options for getting the growth back on track. They charged Trend Micro millions of dollars to find the best answer, and they came up with a proximity move: get closer to the customer by segmenting the entire company into three units. These business units would be based on customer buying behavior and staffed with general managers to assess the market and build the right products for their respective units.

The entire company of three thousand people was reorganized, and we spent the next eighteen months making changes and building products for consumers, small and medium business (SMB), and enterprise (customers with more than one thousand employees). In the buildup to launching our new SMB product, the GM, Steve Quane, described how committed his team was to serving the SMB segment. He told a story to the entire sales team about a recent surfing trip he'd taken to Bali. He described the waves as "epic." Too epic. Big waves cause injuries. They can even kill.

Quane is married, by the way, has two kids, and was probably way too old to be taking so much risk. But he did it anyway because, screw it, if you're going to die, you might as well die doing something you love. Now, you might think this was reckless, but it certainly wasn't timid. Quane's point was that we were going to serve the SMB market the right way, or we were going to die trying. We weren't going to sit on the fence and play it safe. Quane demanded that we burn the boats on the old strategy and go all in on the new strategy. The other GMs followed suit.

It worked. The company returned to high growth shortly after. By 2009 they had grown to $1 billion and added $4 billion in market cap due to this proximity move. I helped drive that growth forward by adding more mass to the inner core through the introduction of cloud-based security technologies. This strategy became known as the Smart Protection Network. Ten years later, it's still alive and well. And like I said earlier, this book is about how all the shots go together. None of this success would have been possible if not for the best leadership team I've ever been a part of, so hats off to my friends Eva, Steve, Mahendra, Lane, Carol, Susan, John, Punit, Q, and our friend Raimund Genes, a true Shot Caller. Rest in peace, brother.

Here's the prescription to this strategy trap. It's simple: burn the damn boats and commit to proximity strategies that honor the Three *R*s. If you keep failing the test, there's a good chance you are close but not close enough to your customer.

All's Fair in Love and War

The Opposing Gravity Grid helps you understand how much opposing gravity you're competing against. The idea is to apply as much (or more) antigravity to offset that force. You compete against fierce competition and against customers who are perfectly happy to simply do nothing. Doing nothing has a lot of mass!

If I asked you to describe your antigravity strategy, what would you say? Probably not much, because antigravity strategies are woefully underutilized. The trap for antigravity strategy is simple—antigravity strategies rarely go far enough. We've all seen the classic battle card, a grid contrasting features between your offer and your competitors' offers. They're a snooze fest. You need to be bold and not afraid to offend the market. I've always believed in the products I was selling, and I always felt I let my target customer down when they didn't buy my product. My job was to pass the Three *R*s test, and when I lost a deal or a customer, I failed the test.

Here's the prescription for antigravity. Use it. Attack the inner core of your competition. Don't beat around the bush or just focus on price, go after their inner core. If you're soft on knowledge of how to attack the inner core of your opposing gravity, you have a weakness that must be addressed. Build this competency because it's worth it.

Don't be a whiner or a coward. Customers do not want to hear your *opinion* about their alternatives. They want insight. You must invest the resources necessary to give them legitimate commentary about the other alternatives they're considering. Don't think that using antigravity is somehow beneath you. That's just being a coward. Antigravity will save your customer from making a mistake.

The Rest is History

How many times have you heard a story that spun a series of events, actions, behaviors, reactions, and so on that didn't entirely add up? But somehow the storyteller wrapped it all up with the phrase "the rest is history." This implies that no one knows why this amazing outcome came to be. It just happened. Or worse, some Kabuki Dancer claims that it all happened for some bullshit reason that makes no sense.

That's the trap with super gravity. It's easy to believe that the world will rally to your cause. That network effect will burst out of your innovation. Feelings of goodwill will latch onto your brand. Value chains will emerge that can't wait to participate.

Guess again. Super gravity is like the business version of a miracle. Conditions have to be just right for it to occur, and even then, luck, timing, effort, and resources are all critical to have a chance at creating super gravity. There's no real trick here. Super gravity is hard to achieve, but you increase your chances of creating it if you avoid these traps:

The **network effect** requires critical mass, plain and simple. Any innovation that's depending on this form of super gravity needs to know that number (check out Metcalfe's law to figure that out). There's a dangerous belief that you can simply go viral. It doesn't work like that. Network effects will only occur if the participants are receiving enough value to engage and stay engaged. Otherwise they never materialize, or they fizzle out over time.

Zero barrier, delayed reward isn't as hard because it's easy to give away something of value. Humans are pretty good at consuming valuable stuff that doesn't cost them anything. The trick is converting that delayed reward into an actual reward. Don't get trapped into getting so good at giving something away that you never get paid for it.

The brutal reality of the **value chain** is that it takes a lot of money to establish and control. This form of super gravity is pretty much reserved for big and powerful companies. There are examples where your offer can become part of a supply chain, which can produce tremendous success, but that's not super gravity. The reality of this form of super gravity is that all participants must accept that they are giving up some of their gravity as the price to participate. This is not easily agreed to or managed, so don't get in over your head trying to build value chains unless you are extremely confident you can pull it off.

Houston, We Have a Problem

Orbit is awesome. It means your customers keep circling your offer, buying, and renewing over and over. They're happy, you're happy, everyone is happy. So what could possibly go wrong?

Orbits decay over time. This means your gravity actually weakens in the mind of the customer. Someone will come along with a solution that gets the job done better or at a lower price. Then that opposing gravity will rip your customer out of your orbit and into theirs.

This is both inevitable and predictable, but unfortunately most companies fall into the "Houston, we have a problem" trap. That's the famous radio communication from the astronauts on the *Apollo 13* mission to Mission Control in Houston, Texas, after a major malfunction turned their mission from a voyage to the moon to a survival mission. It's also what happens when your customers stop buying or start switching to alternatives. The Kabuki Dancers all start panicking, like somehow it's an emergency that no one could have possibly seen coming. These knee-jerk reactions can sometimes make it even worse by giving away hard-earned gravity to compensate for slowing growth. Big mistake.

So why does this happen? It's usually because Shot Callers are not in charge. When orbits decay or opposing gravity occurs, people don't see it coming or don't have the experience to get ahead of it in the first place. The incentive system for many companies doesn't align with dealing with this trap. Too often, there's more incentive to *defer* dealing with it, so people wait until the wolf is ringing the doorbell before they do something about it.

I have experienced both of these situations. This trap appeared at nearly every company I worked at. At Trend Micro, we owned the web security gateway. I mean, we literally owned it because we held the actual patent for scanning web traffic for viruses. Don't worry if you don't know what that means. The important thing is, virtually every major enterprise was using our product because of the patent. We had the most incredible list of blue-chip customers you could ever dream of having.

Around and around they went, orbiting our solution, renewing their contracts, paying us a fortune. Then one day, I got a call from one of my top sales reps, Tom Preiss, who handled our big financial services customers in NYC. "Houston, we have a problem." OK, that's not exactly what he said, but he may as well have. "Morgan Stanley is kicking us out and going with Blue Coat." Don't worry about who Blue Coat is; the important thing is they had mass out the ass and we didn't. They had a product that was far superior, and our patent wasn't going to protect us.

You may be thinking, *Dude, you should've seen this coming*. I did. And when I reported it up the chain of command, guess what happened? Nothing. The product team (which I was eventually put in charge of) had no answers. Three months later, we lost ten more blue-chip customers. By year's end, it was game over. The market we had once dominated was gone.

Here's the prescription: Protect the inner core at all costs! The only way to do this is to stay completely honest about whether or not you are passing the Three *R*s Test. Competition doesn't pop up out of nowhere. They are right in front of you! Deal with the test early, or you will get the "Houston we have a problem" call.

The Whole Shot Grid

Getting everyone on the same page is by far the most valuable consequence of Shot Calling. I've heard the lament about not being on the same page a thousand times. This process solves it—for good. The Whole Shot Grid also contains the very essence of Shot Calling because it requires you to set targets for everything. Every CEO whose teams produce a Whole Shot Grid has a blueprint for success. All they have to do is manage to the grid, and they win. If anything goes wrong, the blueprint tells you what to fix. Involve your whole company in this process if possible and share the damn grid when done. Create Shot Callers, hold them accountable, and you become unstoppable. Here's a sample grid with guidance for each section.

And you'll notice a line for things you don't know how to construct yet. So keep reading. Trust me—by the time you do your grid in the Whole Shot, you will be astounded by how powerful it makes you feel.

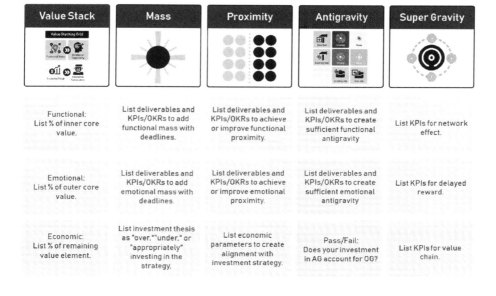

Figure 1.6 The Whole Shot Grid.

THE KILL SHOT

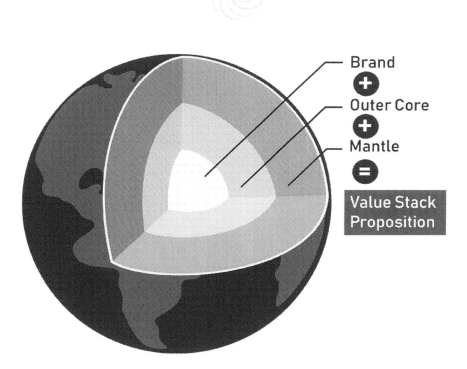

Figure 2.1 Value Stack Proposition (illustrated).

Some time ago, I attended a marketing strategy class at Northwestern University's Kellogg School of Management with a group of executives across many industries. My most useful takeaway was an expression that a professor implored us to remember. He insisted that the most important job of any marketer was to "lower the cost of customer thinking." This means making it as clear and concise as possible what your offer represents to the marketplace. I've used that idea to guide marketing teams over and over as we've worked on branding, packaging, and messaging. Unfortunately, I don't think my guidance to these teams was that helpful. As much as I wanted to, I didn't know how to lower the cost of customer thinking. Until now.

Take a look at the illustration above. The best way I can describe the Kill Shot is depicted here. It speaks directly to how to understand what brand (inner core) is and how to arrive at your value stack proposition (brand + outer core + mantle = value stack proposition). Notice how I did not say "value proposition"? That's because the thinking on value proposition has been misleading all along. Why would you treat all value types as equal when they are not? Let's fix this right now by changing the expression to "value stack proposition." Once you understand the linkage between brand and value stack, you are equipped to lower the cost of customer thinking.

There is a reason you're learning about this after you've built your Moonshot. That reason should be clear at this point, but let's call it out to reinforce it. **Most of your offer's value comes from your inner core**. Your Moonshot reveals not just your inner core but rather your value stack comprising that inner core, your outer core, and the mantle. This stack represents the essence of how your target customer perceives your value. That's the key to lowering the cost of customer thinking, unlocking the value of your offer, and becoming a marketing Shot Caller. That's what the Kill Shot is all about.

Like the Moonshot, the Kill Shot is a system that breaks down into essential components. For the Kill Shot, those are the following.

- **Brand Promise**: The unique promise of value emanating from your inner core. What's your shortcut to help the target customer understand your inner core's value?
- **Value Stack Proposition**: A statement that effectively describes the three layers of your value stack.
- **Solution-Level Forecasting**: What you expect an offer to pro-

duce, usually in terms of revenue. After all, you can't be a Shot Caller without calling your shot.

- **SAVE (Solution, Access, Value, Educate)**: The new framework to pursue marketing objectives; it replaces the traditional Four *P*s of marketing.
- **Integrated Marketing**: Consensus among and between Shot Callers about how, when, and where marketing strategy gets executed.

To make your Kill Shot, we're going to study each element. Let's start with the components of brand and the role each plays in your Kill Shot. Brand, branding, and brand promise are often confusing, so I'd like to give you the precise definitions I've used for each over the last fifteen years.

Brand

Even if your role doesn't include responsibility for the brand, you still need to learn this. All Shot Callers are responsible for carrying the brand torch and holding themselves and their teams accountable for staying on brand. What the hell does that mean? This: **brand is your unique promise of value**. It's the best definition of brand I've ever heard. It's from a brand expert whose name I can't remember (sorry). I love this definition because, as all Shot Callers know, value comes in three forms. Not surprisingly, brand is a reflection of the three forms of value that always need to be accounted for. Let's break that definition down:

- **Unique**: Speaks directly to your superpower, which comes from your inner core, almost always either functional or emotional. One caution here: if your uniqueness is so complicated that no one will understand it, don't include it in your brand promise statement. You will merely raise the cost of customer thinking rather than lower it. Instead, express your uniqueness in terms of a desirable business outcome, not a description of how that outcome is produced. You'll read some examples shortly that will help you make sense of this.

- **Promise**: Your committed endeavor (mission) is what powers the promise you make to the marketplace. It's all the ways that endeavor adds up to a promise you can keep. This should reflect your outer core value. Examples to follow.
- **Value**: Speaks to the worthiness of an offer. You could literally replace "unique promise of value" with "unique promise of worthiness." However, it's critically important to understand your value stack and not misguide the marketplace here. Unless your inner core is "emotional satisfaction," it's often best to keep allusions of worthiness out of your brand or brand promise statement. Instead, focus on the outcomes produced by your offer. Same here, examples to follow.

In a few pages, we're going to break down brand promises to see if they check all the brand boxes. Before that, though, we need to talk about the most common misconceptions about brands.

Misconception 1: Brand Versus Branding

We need a quick detour from the idea of a brand to make something clear. *Brand* is not the same as *Branding*. The point of "big *B*" Branding is to **create shortcuts** that establish an association between your inner core and your offer. Branding can also be used to establish an association between your vision or mission and your company or offer. Branding at that level is not appropriate for anyone except the biggest companies, especially those with a business-to-consumer (B2C) focus.

The CEO of a $10 billion dollar company once told me, "Honestly, I don't give a shit about branding. I only care about the relevance of the brand." I've never forgotten that conversation because it taught me how to think about the power of relevance over branding.

Misconception 2: Branding Versus Relevance

The beauty of Shot Calling is that executing all the shots automatically creates relevance for your offer or organization. The market will remember and reward you if you have gravity. Spending on pure "branding" isn't a good investment for most businesses because most offers are too complex for a single image or idea to permeate the collective consciousness of the marketplace. Giant consumer product companies like Coke or Pepsi do it because chips and soda are pretty simple. That's nearly impossible for most complex offers. Instead, pursue relevance through Shot Calling. Let me tell you a story about what happens when you don't.

In June 2016, a NASCAR racing team reached out to Malwarebytes CMO Rebecca Kline. Would we like to sponsor one of their cars? An odd request considering Malwarebytes wasn't a megacorporation that sells consumer goods like most other NASCAR sponsors do. Sure, Malwarebytes had a solid B2C business, but nothing close to Busch Beer, GEICO, or Xfinity. So why us? Feel free to google the full story. Here's my summary.

The NASCAR team had been attacked by a hacker with ransomware. In this type of attack, a hacker encrypts the files on the victim's computer and blackmails them into paying a ransom to de-encrypt the files. The racing team's files contained years' worth of telemetry data on the car, valued at millions of dollars. The team paid the ransom and got their data back. Whew. Then they removed the malicious attacker software from the computer using Malwarebytes. End of story.

Not quite. The clever marketing guy from the NASCAR team contacted Rebecca, told her the story, and pitched the sponsorship idea. They would do as much press, media, and branding as we wanted. All we had to do was pony up $500,000, and we'd get a 25 percent sponsorship, meaning the car would feature Malwarebytes graphics every fourth race. It was an amazing story. The sponsorship seemed like it would add gravity, so we did it.

Sure, we got some great press and had a blast hanging out with the NASCAR team, but this branding strategy didn't move the needle. At all. Remember, the purpose of branding is to create shortcuts to your inner core. Complex offers are hard to shortcut. That's why branding strategies are typically not smart investments for tech companies. Google and Microsoft were both NASCAR sponsors but aren't anymore. For most businesses, my marketing guidance is to **seek relevance through effective gravity moves**. Branding isn't one of them. Leave that to Coke and Pepsi.

Brand Promise

Let's get back to brand. A brand is your unique promise of value. This definition leads directly to brand promise. Some say there is a difference between a brand promise and a brand statement. Ignore them. These are the same for all practical purposes.

Brand promise is exactly what it sounds like—**a statement to the market that expresses the core value of your brand**. Can someone read your brand promise and accelerate their understanding of your value? Does it lower the cost of customer thinking? Let's examine the guidance I use when designing a brand promise statement. This statement should decorate your website, hallways, trade shows, and T-shirts. It should permeate the minds of your employees the same way you want it to permeate the minds of the marketplace. Then let's have some fun and look at examples of both good and bad brand promises. Then it's your turn: you'll write the brand promise statement for your offer. Follow this guidance and you'll be on your way to being a marketing Shot Caller.

Brand Promise Statement Guidance

A brand promise statement will be effective if it meets this guidance. It should honor the definition of brand—unique promise of value. This is not to say that this guidance replaces the creative aspects of writing; good writing always helps. As you would imagine, this works from the inside out, so let's start with the inner core.

1. Reflect the <u>uniqueness</u> of your inner core. This is accomplished two ways. First, if your inner core can be described concisely, in ten words or fewer, it's best to describe it. However, there is a line you must not cross where the description becomes too complex. You risk losing mindshare if you cross that line. You will *raise* rather than lower the cost of customer thinking. Any time you make it harder to buy your stuff, that's bad marketing. Instead, write a statement that gives the buyer an expectation of the outcome your offer produces. The examples you're about to read will make this easy to understand.

2. Reflect the <u>promise</u> your offer makes to the marketplace. This promise should feel like your mission. Remember the definition of mission? "Committed endeavor." Think about all the work, sweat, tears, drama, joy, stress, money, and time you and your company poured into your endeavor—all of it for the sole purpose of being able to make a promise to your target customer. Your uniqueness is what creates your ability to make a promise to the marketplace. The promises you make are manifestations of that uniqueness. They always fall into two categories: advantages gained and peril avoided. A great brand promise forms a relationship between uniqueness and the promises made about the advantage to be gained or peril to be avoided. Of course you have to be able to rationalize or resolve these promises, or it's all for naught.

3. Reflect the <u>worthiness</u> of your offer. This is your remaining value element. Oftentimes it's economic value, but not always. Be careful—imploring the marketplace to internalize your offer's worthiness within your brand statement is risky. That's because markets are fluid. One day you're the new kid on the block with an offer that's very worthy. The next day you're not due to cir-

cumstances beyond your control. Pinning worthiness to your brand can make it fragile. So unless your inner core is emotional satisfaction or economic value, it's best to leave statements about worthiness to your value stack proposition. That's where you fully flesh out your value stack anyway, so don't make your brand unnecessarily fragile if you don't have to.

4. Lower the cost of customer thinking. This is the most important test of any brand promise statement. Your statement needs to advance the target buyer's comprehension of your offer. It doesn't have to bring full comprehension; that's what your value stack proposition will do. But it sure as hell can't make it less clear. Keep working if yours does because customers are not going to figure it out for you.

We cannot move off this subject without touching on the guidance that you'll face if you're at a big company or become a big company. What do you do when you have a broad portfolio of offerings? How do you unify those under a single brand statement? Here's my guidance:

1. If your value consists of a collection of offerings, you are a "platform of value" and should seek a position in the marketplace as a platform. This is the most common form of positioning for companies with many offers. They seek to convince the market of the power of the platform. Your brand promise statement should reflect that positioning. However, nothing else changes. You must still write a brand statement that reflects your unique promise of value, but it must reflect the aggregate value of the platform, not the individual value of the component pieces.

2. If your value consists of a collection of cores, you must create brand promise statements for each. Google Alphabet is a good example of a collection of cores. Remember, core is discrete. Each core must have its own Moonshot and Kill Shot. Any brand promise statement about a collection of cores should reflect the overall vision of the driving force behind the collection.

Remember, vision reflects "aspirational good." A brand statement at that level should speak to the aspirational good that the collection of cores can produce. Don't expect it to lower the cost of customer thinking. That's not the point. Rather, think of it as a unifying statement that provides the marketplace with a sense of how and why the cores go together. This is a Fortune 100 branding exercise.

Brand Promise Examples

Let's break down some well-known brand promise statements and test them against the guidance you just read about. I'll use a variety of examples. At the end, I'll propose differing brand promise statements for one of the most anticipated new products in history, the 2020 Chevy Corvette. That example should bring brand promise statements into clarity for anyone who has lingering questions. Then it's your turn to write your brand promise statement and get one step closer to becoming a Shot Caller.

BMW: "The Ultimate Driving Machine." This is my favorite example because it checks all the boxes. And I own several. Value Stack = Functional, Emotional, Economic.

- Reflects Uniqueness: "Ultimate" speaks directly to brand uniqueness. Check.
- Reflects Promise: "Driving Machine" speaks to the mission statement—the committed endeavor. It's not a car. It's not a vehicle. It's a "machine." It's German, and it kicks ass every time. Check.
- Reflects Worthiness: BMW correctly makes no allusion to worthiness in this statement. Check.
- Lowers the Cost of Customer Thinking: Absolutely. This statement makes it totally clear what the offer is all about.

Emailage: "The Global Hub of Email Risk Intelligence." I suggested changing this brand promise after our new Digital Identity product launched but took it back because there was no need. It still nailed it. Value Stack = Functional, Emotional, Economic.

- Reflects Uniqueness: "Global Hub" speaks to exclusiveness, i.e., uniqueness. Check.
- Reflects Promise: "Email Risk Intelligence" speaks exactly— and I mean exactly—to the inner core of the offer. Check, check, check.
- Reflects Worthiness: Emailage correctly leaves any reference to worthiness out of this statement. Check.
- Lowers the Cost of Customer Thinking: Yes, this statement adds comprehension about the offer. Check.

Trend Micro: "250+ million endpoints. 500,000+ companies worldwide. One security software company." It's not hard to understand what Trend Micro is going for here, but let's see if it passes the test. Value Stack = Functional, Emotional, Economic.

- Reflects Uniqueness: There is nothing unique. It only implies uniqueness. Not a complete fail but not great.
- Reflects Promise: "One security software company" with "250+ million endpoints" and "500,000+ companies worldwide." This is reflective of Trend Micro's mission, although it's not that clear what's being promised. Not a complete fail but not great.
- Reflects Worthiness: Trend Micro implies worthiness by referencing its massive install base. This is an assumptive expression of worthiness, not a direct expression. Therefore, it's not adding a lot of mass. A more specific reference of worthiness would have added more mass (i.e., "90 percent of the Fortunate 100 use Trend Micro.")
- Lowers the Cost of Customer Thinking: This statement does not achieve this.

CrowdStrike: "We stop breaches." CrowdStrike and Cylance have remarkably similar offers. Notice the difference in uniqueness. Value Stack = Functional, Emotional, Economic.

- Reflects Uniqueness: Yes, but this promise of peril avoided is an outcome manifested by uniqueness. The technical uniqueness is too complex to include in a brand promise statement. CrowdStrike correctly alludes to outcome instead of a confusing description that would raise, not lower, the cost of customer thinking.
- Reflects Promise: One hundred percent check.
- Reflects Worthiness: CrowdStrike correctly excludes worthiness from their brand promise statement.
- Lowers the Cost of Customer Thinking: I can't think of a more precise way to say this. This is a strong yes.

Cylance: "We stop malware with math." Cylance was sold for just over $1 billion. CrowdStrike has a valuation north of $22 billion. You tell me the difference. Hint: look at the uniqueness. Value Stack = Functional, Emotional, Economic.

- Reflects Uniqueness: Yes, this speaks to "advantage gained" and it includes a description of how. To a cybersecurity professional, "math" refers to artificial intelligence and algorithms. Cylance is clear that their uniqueness is the technique, unlike Crowd-Strike, which makes no reference to the technology behind their uniqueness.
- Reflects Promise: Yes, check. It's a promise they keep.
- Reflects Worthiness: Cylance correctly makes no reference to worthiness.
- Lowers the Cost of Customer Thinking: Yes. However, there are going to be customers who don't comprehend this statement. This is not uncommon when being descriptive about how your offer creates value, especially when your offer is complex.

Arby's: "We have the meats." We go from cybersecurity to an ubiquitous consumer product, fast food. Thus, the value stack is different. So is each element of the brand promise statement. Value Stack = Emotional (Satisfaction), Economic, Functional.

- Reflects Uniqueness: The inner core uniqueness is emotional satisfaction. When you're hankering for meat that's fast, cheap, and pretty good and provides bang for the buck. Boom, that's—Arby's. You're satisfied. Check.
- Reflects Promise: Arby's is promising you that you'll be satisfied with their offer—"the meats"—at the price they charge. And you are. Check.
- Reflects Worthiness: Having "the meats" is a way of communicating that this is not a fancy, high-end offer. Everyone knows Arby's is fast food, so it's clear, just like with all fast food, that economic value is the outer core. Fast food companies, including Arby's, generally do a good job of reaffirming economic value. Check.
- Lowers the Cost of Customer Thinking: Extremely good. There is literally zero ambiguity about this brand promise statement.

The 2020 Chevy Corvette rocked the automotive industry in early 2020 by releasing the first midengine Corvette in history. This means the engine is now in the back of the car. That change, along with many other improvements, created tremendous mass for a car that already had pretty good mass in the first place. It was so dramatically improved that it immediately drew comparisons to supercars costing two to five times more. The interesting part is the value stack for this car. With apologies to anyone not that interested in cars, I think you'll easily grasp the power of turning your value stack into a brand promise statement by using this example.

The biggest idea to remember is how powerful it can be to do this correctly. Chevy can add tremendous gravity simply by making the right promise to each of the three target customers in its stack. Conversely, they can lose gravity if they make the wrong promise to the marketplace or if they try to be everything to everybody by grid jumping. I am pulling this information directly from Chevy's website. Let's run through it and imagine that, at the end, it's up to you to decide. I'll tell you what I would do. What would you do?

2020 Chevy Corvette Value Stack #1: Functional–emotional superiority–economic. The target customer is the buyer who primarily values the functional attributes of the offer. They want functional "bang." Chevy starts with this statement: "Precision is our starting line." This statement checks all the boxes, especially with the word precision, which implies the highest order of functional prowess. "Starting line" is a clear reference to auto racing, implying racecar-level performance. Nicely done for appealing to the buyer attracted to this value stack.

2020 Chevy Corvette Value Stack #2: Emotional superiority–functional–economic. Chevy appeals to the buyer of this stack by saying the new Corvette is a "mid-engine masterpiece." I love how this honors the principle of stacking, alluding to the emotion of owning a masterpiece while including a reference to the functional outer core of the product, the midengine design. Excellent!

2020 Chevy Corvette Value Stack #3: Emotional satisfaction–economic–functional. Since its inception, the Corvette has had appeal as the "poor person's supercar." It's the worst part of their brand in my opinion, but it can easily be fixed. Right now, the Chevy website doesn't try to appeal to this value stack other than displaying the car's price on the first image you see on their website. Pricing adds immense mass for Corvette because it's amazingly low for the performance delivered. This is the quintessential "bang for buck" positioning that many companies covet, but is it right for Corvette? They're in a perfect position to take advantage of it but seem hesitant because of a stigma associated with this value stack, i.e., the "poor person's supercar." This car starts at $60,000 and can easily go over $100,000, so it's not cheap, but it's also not a Porsche or Ferrari, it's a Chevy.

So what brand promise statement would you make about the Corvette if it were up to you? Here's where Shot Calling leads me: The Corvette inner core is emotional satisfaction, so Shot Calling dictates Value Stack #3. Sure, this new car is awesome, and it just might be a masterpiece. But all along, Chevy was committed to delivering the vehicle for under $60,000. That settles it. The strategy was always to give buyers the best performance for the money. And they succeeded. In terms of brand promise statement, here's where it gets extremely exciting. Without changing a single thing on the vehicle, Chevy can:

1. Double down on the Corvette value stack and create a brand promise statement that makes it clear what their offer represents to the marketplace. Something like "Corvette—freakishly worth it." This speaks to the inner core without beating around the bush yet leaves the door wide open to explain why it's "freakishly" worth it. This statement accurately reflects Chevy's mission for this product—and remember, brand promise statements should always reflect a sense of the company's mission. I could see this brand promise carrying Corvette for the next fifty years.

2. Present all three value stacks to the marketplace through segmentation. This means different brand promises to each. This is achievable only if Chevrolet can create the necessary proximity strategies to access each segment. Otherwise, they risk losing gravity due to the value trap you read about earlier, grid jumping. Trying to be everything to everybody doesn't lower the cost of customer thinking, it increases it.

So what would you do? Choose option #1 and risk alienating certain segments of buyers? Or choose option #2 and risk losing gravity through grid jumping? All day and twice on Sunday, I would stick to the stack and choose option #1. This new Corvette is freakishly worth it. That's why I might buy one. That promise reflects mission, is true to the inner core, offers significant opportunities to increase gravity, and, most importantly, lowers the cost of customer thinking.

My Brand Promise Statement

I'd like you to read something.

Shot Calling is a uniquely workable approach for demystifying the universal laws of business, creating winning strategy, unlocking value, unifying teams, avoiding peril, and making you unstoppable.

That's my brand promise statement for this book. Honestly, I don't know where this endeavor will lead, so I have work to do on my Moonshot. But Shot Calling is my innovation, it creates my inner core, it sets my value stack, and it leads me to this brand promise statement. Let's put it to the test. Do I check all the boxes? I'll fire my own ass if I don't. By the way, my value stack is functional–emotional superiority–economic.

- Reflects Uniqueness: As far as I know, Shot Calling is unique on the planet. It did not exist until I created it. No other system will demystify the universal laws of business and unlock value. Hell, there is no other system that attempts to define the universal laws of business, let alone demystify them. The system is the key to unlocking value, another aspect of what makes it unique. Notice that this is outcome based, not descriptive. That's because Shot Calling is complex, and describing how it works would not lower the cost of customer thinking. And when I read this statement, I see my mission in the mirror. This checks the box. I get to keep my job for now.

- Reflects Promise: "Making you unstoppable" is the most bold promise I can make. It speaks directly to your emotional need to feel superior. What's superior to being unstoppable? Nothing! This checks the box big-time. I get to keep my job.

- Reflects Worthiness: This statement makes no reference to worthiness. It implies it, but there is no need to suggest how much it would cost. Books are not expensive. Anyone sweating the cost of the book given what it promises is not my target customer. This passes the test, so I still keep my job.

- Lowers the Cost of Customer Thinking: I give myself a passing grade here, but I am not convinced the cost of customer thinking can't be even lower. So I will do two things. First, I won't fire myself. Second, I will send a $500 gift card to the first reader of this book who creates a brand promise statement for my system that passes this section of the test better than my statement does. All true Shot Callers are always trying to get it right. We're not worried about *always* being right.

Brand Promise Statement Wizard

Once you get good at writing brand promises, you'll add a lot of value to your company. I can't tell you how many bad brand promises I've seen over the years. If people use this wizard just the way it is, ninety-nine out of a hundred brand promises will improve. I have used my own brand promise statement as an example of how this works.

Brand Promise Statement Wizard				Instructions
Unique (Inner Core)	Promise (Mission manifested as outcome aligned to JTBD)	Worthiness (Superior to all alternatives despite the price)	Worthiness (Satisfactory in comparison to all alternatives because of the price)	
Workable system or approach	Demystifying the universal laws of business			Step 1. In column 1, add descriptions of your inner core uniqueness, aka, source of your superpowers.
Democratizes power	Creates winning strategy			Step 2. In column 2, add descriptions of the outcome your customer can expect if you offer delivers on your promise. This outcome should reflect your company mission and address the primary job the customer is trying to get done.
Restores integrity to business	Unifies teams			Step 3. In column 3 (this is optional)- if your worthiness is based on superior outcomes- imply worthiness by amplifying uniqueness, antigravity or consequence for failing to get the job done.
	Unlocks value			Step 4. In column 4- If your worthiness is based on satisfactory outcomes, make a direct reference to economic worthiness.
	Avoid peril			Step 5. Select the superpower that adds the most gravity and put it at the bottom of column 1.
	Make you unstoppable			Step 6. Select the promise of outcome that adds the most gravity and put that at the bottom of column 2.
Super Power that adds the most gravity	Promise that adds the most gravity	Worthiness: Amplify mass, antigravity or consequence	Worthiness: Amplify economic advantage	Step 7. Select the element of worthiness (superpower, antigravity, consequence or economic advantage) that adds the most gravity and put them at the bottom of columns 3 and 4 respectively.
Workable approach	All are in scope for my offer	No statement needed	N/A	Step 8. Combine your "unique promise of worthiness' into a single sentence that concisely and creatively captures each element.
Brand Promise Statement				
Shot Calling is a uniquely workable approach for demystifying the universal laws of business, creating winning strategy, unlocking value, unifying teams, avoiding peril, and making you unstoppable.				

Value Stack Proposition

Flow, baby, flow. That's Shot Calling. Innovation creates value, value creates mass, mass creates gravity, gravity drives strategy, strategy reveals brand promise, and brand promise sets the stage for value stack proposition, the final component of your message before you bring it to the market.

Value stack proposition emerges from brand promise, but it's more comprehensive. While brand promise is designed to emphasize your uniqueness, value stack proposition should convey the value of your entire stack. A good value stack proposition reinforces uniqueness and also includes the gravity moves in play for your offer: mass, proximity, antigravity, and super gravity. Simply put, show me all the ways you've got mass out the ass in a couple of sentences.

Expect the majority of your content strategy to map to your value stack proposition. Most bad value stack propositions make the same mistake as a bad brand promise statement. They raise rather than lower the cost of customer thinking. The last thing in the world you want to do is put something in there that causes your target customer to become skeptical or unnecessarily feel emotions that you then need to resolve before they buy. You always have to pass the Three Rs Test whenever value is exchanged. Do not increase your own burden when creating your value stack proposition by adding things that make it harder to pass the Three Rs Test.

Here's some guidance on how to create a winning value stack proposition. Map it to your Whole Shot Grid. All of your gravity is already accounted for there. The trick is to add the elements that increase gravity without making it harder to pass the Three Rs Test. Let's run through it:

1. **Reiterate your brand promise**. A good brand promise is mostly about your inner and outer core. That's where most of your value is contained, so it's the best starting point. If you focused on the outcomes produced by your inner core instead of descriptions of how it works, this is the place to elaborate with more descriptive messaging.

2. **Account for proximity that adds value**. Be a little careful with this one. Not every proximity move adds value to customers. Sometimes it's just to help you win. Include references to proximity only if they are intended to convey value to customers. A good example is adding "access to experts" as a proximity move. Becoming a trusted advisor by providing specialized resources to customers is another good example. But proximity moves that mostly benefit you and not the customer should not be referenced in your value stack proposition. For example, if you hire salespeople that have no special value to the customer, don't reference access to salespeople as a benefit of exchanging value. No one will care and it won't add gravity.

3. **Add antigravity**. Every value stack proposition must include a reference that weakens the gravity of alternatives. I consider this a rule of Shot Calling. The easiest way to weave this in is to simply include the words "unlike alternatives . . ." Then just complete the sentence in a way that weakens the gravity of alternatives.

4. **Include the value of any super gravity strategy in play**. Just remember that network effect and delayed reward are of obvious value to customers. Value chain strategies sometimes reward the participants more than the customers. So only include a reference here if it adds gravity.

5. **Evaluate it against the Three *R*s Test**. Keep working until it passes. In a perfect world, you'd pass the Three *R*s Test simply because you bring your value into proximity with your customer.

I included many examples of brand promise statements, but for a value stack proposition, I'm just going to use one that I am intimately familiar with. Mine. Here it goes.

Shot Calling is a uniquely workable approach for demystifying the universal laws of business, creating winning strategy, unlocking value, unifying teams, avoiding peril, and making you unstoppable. It teaches you the five shots that make success possible:

- The Moonshot teaches you the realities of how humans perceive value so you can create an effective value stack. It also provides a framework for understanding how to unlock that value by understanding the power of business gravity, the force that shapes markets and determines outcomes. You will learn to manipulate this gravity in your favor by using the Whole Shot Grid to maximize your chance of success. It also teaches you my exclusive list of traps that undermine success, allowing you to avoid peril and move faster with more confidence.
- The Kill Shot will teach you how to translate your value stack into the most effective brand promise and value stack proposition possible. You'll then learn the best way to bring your offer to market and succeed.
- The Money Shot will teach you how to replicate the success of the world's top salespeople.
- The Three-Point Shot will unlock your leadership purpose and teach you how to be a great leader.
- The Whole Shot is all about unifying teams to achieve a common purpose. Success!

Unlike other business books, *Call Your Shots* covers it all using a fresh, exciting approach that anyone can learn. Let this be your go-to business book and let *Call Your Shots* make you unstoppable!

This is a little long, but that's OK because Shot Calling is a very complex offer. But does it pass the guidance? Let's check.

- **Does it reflect brand promise?** Yes, the brand promise statement is how it starts. Notice how it blends in descriptions along with outcomes. This highlights how value stack propositions are different from brand promise statements.
- **Does it account for proximity?** Yes, in that no proximity value is present. Therefore, it's appropriate not to make reference to it.
- **Does it use antigravity?** Yes, using the "unlike" approach.
- **Does it account for super gravity?** Yes, in that no super gravity strategy is in play for Shot Calling, so no mention is made.

- **Does it pass the Three *R*s Test?** Yes, functional value is rationalized through words like *teach*, *learn*, *system*, *translate*, which are all highly functional in nature. Words like *unstoppable*, *demystifying*, *great*, and *confidence* are all highly emotional in nature, chosen to elicit feelings of superiority.

Creating a great value stack proposition isn't hard if you honor the guidance and stick to the stack! Could this be better? Yes! That's the power of knowing how to do this. I can manipulate gravity by changing this statement without changing my offer. Maybe my target customer changes, or my inner core gets more refined. I can change how humans perceive my value without doing anything except changing how I stack value.

Now it's your turn! You've written a brand promise statement. Now try writing a value stack proposition.

Solution-Level Forecasting

On the big product management and product marketing teams I've run, I kept witnessing the same problem. No product- or solution-level forecast from the product manager, product marketers, or even the CMO or CPO (chief product officer). I once asked a product team to produce a product-level forecast. The response?

"What's that?"

When I hire a salesperson, I know how much production to expect, i.e., revenue. I also factor in their ramp time, i.e., how long we have to pay them until they get onboarded and start earning their keep. I use this information to calculate that salesperson's quota.

If the sales team is forecasting revenue, why would marketers need to forecast revenue too? Here's why. Salespeople are tired of taking a knife to a gun fight! If you don't know how much revenue your product is likely to produce, what are the odds it's something with enough mass to move the needle? The answer is horrifying. More than 90 percent of new product innovations fail. That means a lot of pain for everyone involved. The obvious solution is to build products with tons of mass in the first place. Sorry, but that guidance isn't really workable. You should know by now that I recommend implementing a scientific innovation process like ODI to build solutions that have mass from the start. But for most of us, we are stuck with whatever our company has produced or is going to continue to produce using the same methodology that's already in place. So we are also stuck with the "market what you have" or "sell what you have" mentality that Kabuki Dancers love to shovel.

The Three *R*s Test is the best way I know to increase the odds of success. Please, pretty please, with a cherry on top, if you have the authority to include people in designing the Moonshot, do it. Include everyone, because that's how to get everyone on the same page, and that's where accountability begins. The Moonshot isn't complete until the connection between strategy and results is projected. This projection creates the relationship between results and product/solution-level performance. It's basic math, but it's the powerful superglue that binds cause to effect. It also separates Shot Callers from Kabuki Dancers.

Product/solution-level forecasting is not hard. It's only hard to be accurate. For example, let's say it's your job to teach a bunch of third-graders selling ice cream how to make a forecast. The kids' forecast focuses on one question and one question only: **How much ice cream will they sell?** The answer is basically a product-level forecast. The third-graders have to account for several factors. How many kids are in the school? A hundred. How many like ice cream? Half. How many are your targets? Fifty. How many do you think eat ice cream? Half want ice cream every day. OK, so you could sell twenty-five ice cream cones a day. What else do the kids need to consider? How about how many kids want ice cream during recess when it's being sold? What about the cold months when kids want warm cookies? And flavors? What are the preferences for vanilla, chocolate, and strawberry? Are any of those twenty-five customers allergic to dairy? How many of their parents are vegan? Solution-level forecasts go from stupid-simple to extreme complexity the more factors you add. The more you run them, the better you get. It's the Shot Caller's way. Build that muscle because it's amazing how much better you will build your solutions if you do.

Let me be clear. I don't blame marketers for not being able (or wanting) to produce a solution-level forecast. Why would they? Revenue forecasts add tremendous pressure and put people on the hook for results, not just activity. I've been on both sides of this equation. I've owned the teams that had to innovate, build, and bring solutions to market. And I've owned the teams that had to sell those very solutions. Here's what I've learned. If you don't have an accurate sense of what your product or solution can produce in terms of revenue, don't build it.

Products or solutions that have mass are not hard to spot. I quit an $800K a year job as president of Trend Micro to join ZScaler, and I got fired because we couldn't sell enough. Did I believe for one second that cloud computing or cloud security wasn't going to be huge? Nope. Did I believe that ZScaler didn't have mass out the ass? Nope, that's why I quit an $800K a year job! Were conditions right for ZScaler in 2012 to create significant gravity? Nope. The lesson here is simple. Do not confuse low mass with poor conditions. Most importantly, understand what you're betting on:

- If your offer is intended to have an immediate impact on the marketplace, you are not betting on conditions. You should have a forecast and you should see immediate results. If you don't, then "fail fast" and reconsider your Moonshot or at least find ways to add more mass to the offer.
- If your offer is a bet on long-term conditions conspiring in your favor, then forge ahead, but be prudent. There's an old expression in Silicon Valley that "more companies die of indigestion than starvation." Betting on conditions to favor your offer can take a really long time. It took ten years for ZScaler, but the reward was and is off the charts.

Note to C-level executives: You guys own this one. Teach your people how to make product/solution-level forecasts, then put your money where their mouth is. Otherwise, don your Kabuki costume and pretend you're adding gravity. You're not.

SAVE

I bet you two things.

1. If I asked you if you've heard of the "Four *P*s of marketing," you would say yes.

2. If I asked what they are, you'd mumble, "Price, packaging, placement, promotion . . . product . . . positioning . . . people, um . . . pizza? Wait, that's eight *P*s!"

Let's forget about the Four *P*s. May they rest in peace. In 2013, I read in *Harvard Business Review* about a new framework that replaces the Four *P*s called SAVE: solution, access, value, and educate.[3] Besides being easier to remember, the acronym is also more applicable to the modern customer journey.

1. **Product** is the sum of its features and functions. **Solution** is what the product *does*.

2. **Price** is the product's cost. **Value** determines whether or not the price is worth it.

3. **Place** is where customers buy the product. **Access** is the entire journey to get there.

4. **Promotion** is buy-it-now marketing. **Education** is helpful information.

When you're all done creating your SAVE plan, you've basically condensed your marketing plan into these four ideas. What's your solution, and how do you describe it? How will customers gain access? How will the marketplace perceive your value based on price? And how do you intend to educate the market?

Let's put the Shot Caller spin on SAVE. Shot Callers know how to account for all four forms of gravity. It should come as no surprise to

---

3   Richard Ettenson, Eduardo Conrado, and Jonathan Knowles. "Rethinking the 4 P's." *Harvard Business Review*, January-February 2013. www.hbr.org/2013/01/rethinking-the-4-ps.

you by now that we can map gravity onto the SAVE framework. Here's how that looks:

- Solution → Mass
- Access → Proximity, Super Gravity (if applicable)
- Value → Three *R*s Test
- Educate → Proximity, Antigravity

Why is this not a surprise? Because whether the creators of the Four *P*s, the Eight *P*s, SAVE, or any other framework realized it or not, *everything* that works in business maps to the four forms of gravity. It's as close to a unifying theory of gravity as you'll ever find. Any idea, strategy, or tactic that doesn't align with business gravity is incomplete or just wrong.

Solution (Mass)

My favorite business book, *What Customers Want*, says that products are tools customers use to get jobs done. Since *all* products are simply solutions to unfinished jobs, we can accurately state that solutions are also tools to help customers get jobs done.

The SAVE framework challenges us to define offers by the needs they meet, not by their features, functions, or advantages. I agree with this strategy for packaging and communicating your solution. It should focus on customer needs, but that doesn't go far enough. Shot Callers know that not all needs are created equal. Many are already well met, so there's strong opposing gravity offsetting your offer's gravity. Remember the Opposing Gravity Grid with its tools and jobs, new and old?

Ideally, your offer brings a new solution to market that addresses a new job for customers, but this situation is so rare that it's hard to come up with examples. In fact, the only example in my career when I've marketed or sold a "new/new" (new tool for a new job) was in cybersecurity when a new form of malware or hacker attacked the world out of nowhere. This sucked for consumers but was awesome for business. I refer to this rare occurrence of new/new as "Camelot."

If your business is ever in Camelot, everything just works. All your marketing, all your activities, all your ideas. Everyone is a genius in Camelot, but it never lasts. The customer job goes from being underserved to being well served. Competitors emit opposing gravity. Whatever uniqueness drove your value stack proposition goes from being amazingly valuable to just somewhat valuable. The pull created by your initial gravity now needs to be replaced with all the other gravity moves. Unfortunately, Camelot is also the "Kabuki Dancers' nursery." The anomalous conditions of Camelot teach false lessons about why things happened the way they did.

I'll never forget the moment when a company I worked for announced that our new mission was to go "back to the future." This was a directive to employees to act the way they used to when we were in our Camelot phase and had mass out the ass. Once we left Camelot, as businesses always do, the CEO longed for the incredible days when everything just worked. Every decision seemed right; every activity seemed to produce a significant return. Who wouldn't want to go back to this future?

It's a natural impulse to seek better days. It's also a trap, and many CEOs, especially founders, fall into it. The reality is you can't go back. You must go forward. So what does that mean? Opposing gravity wins every time if you don't add more inner core mass, right? Wrong! We know that innovation creates value and value creates mass. We also know that value can only be perceived three ways. What you may not know is that **the outcomes your solution creates fall into eight different categories**. This is according to Strategyn, the company that pioneered Outcome-Driven Innovation and "jobs to be done." Here are those eight categories, which can also be thought of as steps to get any job done so the outcome makes the customer feel the necessary emotion, which is either superior or satisfied depending on your value stack.

1. **Define:** Customers determine their goals and plan resources.

2. **Locate:** Customers gather items and information needed to do the job.

3. **Prepare:** Customers set up the environment to do the job.

4. **Confirm:** Customers verify that they're ready to perform the job.

5. **Execute:** Customers carry out the job.

6. **Monitor:** Customers assess whether the job is being successfully executed.

7. **Modify:** Customers make alterations to improve execution.

8. **Conclude:** Customers finish the job or prepare to repeat it.4

You don't have to beat competitors in every category. I've won many deals because my solution delivered high-value job outcomes better than alternatives. My product made the customer feel superior in some categories but not all. That's the point of aligning solutions to outcomes instead of features. Which brings up two questions.

1. How do you know which outcomes are high value and which are low value?

2. How do you know how much opposing gravity you'll face in each category?

Good questions. Hard to answer without data. I've used several market research techniques like MaxDiff, which calculates the maximum differential in value between your features. It's useful to understand which job outcomes are of high value, but it doesn't account for opposing gravity. Outcome-Driven Innovation does both, and I highly recommend the ODI approach. It uses a formula that determines an "**opportunity score**" for customer outcomes. The higher the score, the more valuable it is to help customers achieve said outcome. It works like this:

1. Survey a minimum of 100 customers on how important certain outcomes are. For example, in cybersecurity, you might ask customers, **"How important is it to minimize the likelihood of a**

4   Tony Ulwick. "Outcome-Driven Innovation: JTBD Theory in Practice." JTBD + Outcome-Driven Innovation®. Jun 21, 2017. www.jobs-to-be-done.com/outcome-driven-innovation-odi-is-jobs-to-be-done-theory-in-practice-2944c6ebc40e.

data breach?" ODI uses a 1–5 scale, with 5 being most import-ant and 1 being least important. Let's say 87 percent of survey respondents said that outcome was very important (a score of 4 or 5).

2. Next, using the same example, you would ask, **"How satisfied are you with your current solution for minimizing the like-lihood of a data breach?"** Let's say 42 percent of respondents indicated they were already very satisfied (4 or 5).

3. To calculate the opportunity score, simply express the percent score as a number by moving the decimal. So 87 percent be-comes 8.7, and 42 percent becomes 4.2. Then just follow this formula: **Importance + (Importance – Satisfaction) = Oppor-tunity Score**. In our example, it's 8.7 + (8.7 – 4.2) = 4.5 for a total score of 13.2 (8.7 + 4.5 = 13.2). This is a high score and would indicate a valuable opportunity to pursue. For all the de-tails on ODI, such as what the scores represent, please consult with Strategyn.

For our purposes, we can think of an opportunity score as a "net gravity score." **Your Gravity – Opposing Gravity = Net Gravity**. Same idea. It is extremely important to understand as you put your solu-tions into the market. You can't just focus on what seems important to customers. You have to account for opposing gravity, or there's a pretty good chance you're going to get screwed because customers already feel superior or satisfied. Imagine that in our cybersecurity example, 75 percent of respondents already felt very satisfied. Do the math. 8.7 + (8.7 – 7.5) = 9.9. That's a terrible opportunity score (net gravity score). You could innovate the shit out of everything your product does to achieve that functional outcome, but no one's going to pay for it because it's not meeting an underserved need. If you put all your innovation eggs in that basket, you would lose them all. Those two simple survey questions help you avoid that disaster.

This is what I meant a few paragraphs ago by "data." Unless you are prepared to invest significant time and money in a scientific method like ODI, you are operating without any real understanding of opposing gravity. It's not perfect, but the Opposing Gravity Grid gives you some indication of what you're up against in the marketplace. I've tried to bring ODI into every company I've worked with since first using it at Trend Micro in 2008. Unfortunately, I couldn't overcome the greatest gravitational force in all of business: **the gravity of the status quo**. You will face the same, so get comfortable with the Opposing Gravity Grid. This tool is easy to use and will save you from heartburn.

Solution Packaging Guidelines

In the SAVE framework, solution is all about how you package an offer and present its value to the target customer. By now, you understand the forces at work in your favor and against you. With these in mind, here are some guidelines for packaging your solution.

1. **Solution Name**: Almost everyone reading this should care far more about relevance, not brand awareness. The expression, "We are a branded house, not a house of brands," applies. In other words, *do not create names for solutions, products, or features*. Google spent billions building a cloud solution called Google Cloud. They could have named it something obscure, but they didn't. They named their cloud service "cloud," and they 100 percent got that right.

   At Trend Micro, my team spent $500,000 on packaging consultants to study the best potential names for our security products. Guess what the research showed? That our solutions should be named using descriptors. Just as Google named their cloud solution Google Cloud, we changed the name of our endpoint security product from OfficeScan to Trend Micro Endpoint Security. Hard to believe we paid $500,000 for that lesson. We changed the names of all Trend products from goofy "brands" to simple descriptions. For example, our web security product went from Interscan Virus Wall to Trend Micro Web Security. Sales went up. Don't build brands; stick with descriptors.

2. **Base Offer and Upsell**: I spent a week studying marketing strategy at the Kellogg School of Management at Northwestern University. You now know that value needs to be stacked in order to maximize how well it is perceived. A brilliant professor at Kellogg referred to packaging your value stack as creating "naked solutions, with options." This means to package your solution with a base offer (naked) and create add-ons (options). Hence, naked solution with options. This isn't new, but it's very effective for creating upsell opportunities. The trick is knowing what to put in the base offer and what to offer as an upsell or a premium option. Here are the rules I follow:

   a. The base offer must include your inner core value, and it must be able to resolve the customer's emotional need to feel superior or satisfied. Any additional component that doesn't increase emotional gravity belongs in the base offer. For example, the base model Mercedes better make customers feel superior. It does. It's a Mercedes. But does adding air conditioning increase emotional value or is it really just a base-level feature? Obviously it's a base-level feature and belongs in every base model offer, and it does. You can't even buy a new Mercedes that doesn't have AC in its base offer.

   b. Add-ons or upsell options should only be an additional cost if they help make the customer feel superior. Otherwise, parts of your offer that are just "good enough" to get the job done should be included in the base offer at no extra cost to the customer. Remember that you do *not* need to be superior in all the eight categories identified by Strategyn. In fact, most offers don't give customers a massively delightful, superior experience at every step. The reality is, for most products, the eight categories are a mix of emotional satisfaction and superiority.

To construct your packaging, we are going to blend the eight-category job outcome map from Strategyn with Shot Calling. This will make your life so much easier as you think about how to package your offer. It's this simple. Use the packaging grid as follows:

1. Start with your base offer. That's the job your solution will allow your customer to execute, so it belongs in the "execute" row. Put the name of your base offer in that row.

2. Then go to row 1 (define) and think through how your offer helps your customer determine goals and resources. Use the third column in that row to briefly describe how your solution addresses this job category. Finally, use the fourth column to indicate whether this aspect of your offer will increase emotional gravity enough to make the customer feel superior or merely satisfied. Just type the word superior or satisfied in the fourth column.

3. Proceed with the same approach for each row until you have completed the grid. The word superior or satisfied must be in column 4 for all rows.

4. Package your base-level offer using your base component and any other component that merely achieves satisfied outcomes.

5. Reserve any component that you've indicated as superior as your upsell or add-on components.

That's it! That's all it takes to package your offer for maximum effect. Now it's your turn. Use the packaging grid below and practice creating packaging.

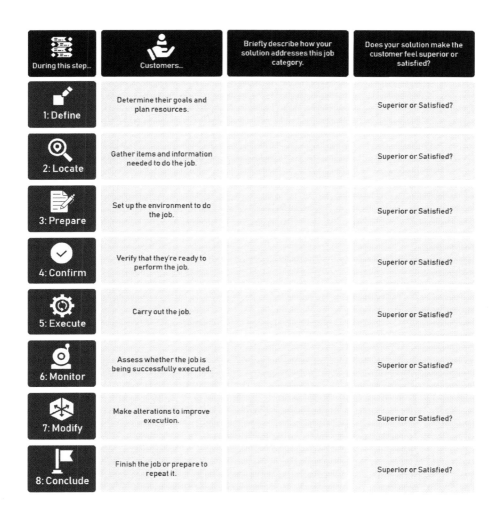

Figure 2.2 Offer packaging grid.

Access (Proximity and Super Gravity)

I took my first Uber ride in 2013 in San Francisco. My good friend Roger Cobb and I were standing in the rain, and Roger "called" an Uber. I've hired Roger as a sales rep at four different companies. He's about as technical as you'll find for a salesperson. He was delighted to show me the Uber app on his phone. I was impressed as most people were the first time they used Uber. Getting a cab in San Francisco sucks compared to NYC, so I was blown away when a town car pulled up within five minutes.

This example illustrates the power of access, the second element of the SAVE framework. Access is simply getting as close as possible to customers with as many ways to meet their needs as you can offer. Here's how Uber did that. Back in 2011, Uber had one ride option. Now they have four and food. At the push of button, you can choose to feel superior with Uber Black or satisfied with UberX. Uber can target you as an "emotional inner core buyer" with Uber Black for status or as a "functional inner core buyer" with UberXL for carrying luggage or multiple passengers. These powerful options reveal the potential of using access to create or manipulate gravity. In Uber's case, there's even value chain super gravity in that drivers who don't work for Uber provide the workforce and equipment necessary to run the business. In exchange, the drivers become business owners, set their hours, and make money on demand.

Another company that nails access is Apple. Apple stores feature this proximity move called the Genius Bar. Think of the decision to brand your *tech support counter*. Instead of dealing with an "associate" you're now talking to a "genius." This access strategy absolutely helps Apple pass the Three *R*s Test and is especially brilliant given Apple's price point in the marketplace.

Throughout my career, I have used every access strategy known to exist, including direct selling, telesales, robocalls, licensing, original equipment manufacturing, retail, mobile apps, reselling, value-added reselling, distribution, value-added distribution, agents, in-product, service provider, cloud, e-commerce, website, freemium, free, infomercial, and probably a few I can't remember. Trust me; if it exists, I've tried it.

Here's everything I've learned about access strategies that work condensed into three guidelines.

1. **Friction is the enemy**. Anything you can do to reduce friction and dissonance in your access strategies improves them. At Trend Micro, we lived by the phrase, "easy to do business with." We had a massively complex channel strategy with over one hundred thousand participants. If we made our products hard to buy, in the immortal words of *Pulp Fiction*'s Jules Winnfield, we were "as dead as fried chicken."

2. **Super gravity strategies always include complex access challenges**. I've seen many failed attempts to create super gravity because the companies were unprepared to deal with this complexity. They didn't take seriously the challenges of creating the win-win outcomes that can only happen if access challenges are addressed. Do not attempt a super gravity strategy if you are not prepared to burn the boats and solve for the complexity that super gravity strategies create regarding access.

3. **Most access strategies have already been used**. The hard part isn't figuring out which access strategy to use (direct sales, mobile app, etc.), so I'm leaving that up to you. The hard part is getting it to work. I've learned that whether your access strategy is designed to improve proximity or create super gravity, the key to success is right above in guidelines one and two. You will rarely, if ever, create a new access paradigm in your entire career. Stick with what works, just make it work for you.

Value (Orbit)

We've discussed value at great length. By now, you understand humans perceive it in three forms and why. There are even more connections between value and gravity that we'll explore in later sections of the book, but for the purposes of SAVE, I want to focus on the relationship between value and pricing.

Remember the guidance on SAVE "Articulate the benefits of your solution relative to price, rather than stressing how price is driven by features, costs, profits, or competition." This is often referred to as **value-based selling**, and it's been in the mainstream for years. Pricing based on value allows you to bring customers into orbit and stay there because they perceive the offer is worth it.

Remember from the Moonshot section that emotional value and economic value have a pretty tight relationship. Maybe your price has created unsettled feelings that this thing isn't worth it. But at a lower price, it's worth it now. I feel superior because compared to alternatives at that price, I bought the best product. What should your pricing strategy be? I've run pricing exercises for many solutions. Here's what I've learned:

1. **Let the market set the price**. Whether for your base offer or your upsell, the market will tell you what to do. Why? Because the market is already under the full force of the gravity of alternatives. It's like betting on horses. The odds already account for the "gravity" of each horse. There's no point in arguing with the oddsmakers. Simply decide how much risk you want to take and place your bet. Pricing is similar. Pick a starting point, which isn't hard; just use common sense. Then see how the market responds.

    When Emailage was about to release a new version of our flagship product, I sat in the room with the chief product officer (CPO) and his team. The question was asked, "How much are we going to charge for it?" The CPO said, "Well, it's twice as good as the previous version." So I asked, "Well, should we charge twice as much?" And the CPO said, "Yeah, we should." That was our starting point, and it was effective. We modified the pricing as needed using discounting and learned that charging twice as much was too ambitious, so we adjusted. Some of you might have the wherewithal to apply more science to your pricing models, and that's fine. Just make sure that no matter whether you're using the back of a napkin or a complicated pricing algorithm that you have the agility to adjust.

2. **Be smart about discounts**. If you rarely have to discount your offer to win, your price is too low for the value. Raise the price. If you do need to discount to win, here's the guidance I've had success with:

   a. When opposing gravity is low, customers react favorably to discounts as low as 5 to 15 percent.

   b. When opposing gravity is strong, customers react favorably to discounts of 25 percent or more.

   c. If you already discount by more than 50 percent on average, your base pricing is delusional. Lower it until average discounting normalizes at no more than 25 percent.

   d. The exception to these guidelines is instances of value inflow where a "land grab" is occurring. To acquire market share, do whatever is necessary to win. Worry about adjusting for better margins and profits down the road. Do not miss out on a land grab, ever.

3. **Remember the Three Rs**. Functional value must be <u>rationalized</u>, emotional value must be <u>resolved</u>, and economic value must <u>reaffirm</u> your offer's worthiness. Don't get boxed into discounting to offset every customer pushback on price. Here's the little trick I use that will guide you every time in terms of the Three Rs Test. Don't ask the customer what they think. Ask them how they feel? If they say "I'm not feeling it," meaning they

have unresolved emotions, you have not succeeded in rationalizing your functional value and need to revert back to doing that. Once they reach the state where all that's necessary is to agree on price, reaffirm the value of your solution by reminding them of the business outcomes only you can deliver. That single question "How are you feeling?" is powerful because it allows you to pivot in any direction.

4. **Don't screw around**. Shot Callers hold people to the highest standard of communicating and proving value. Department, team, and role don't matter. Expect nothing less than a world-class sales call every time someone talks to a customer, or you are leaving money on the table. Salespeople, I love you to death, but if you have a solution with plenty of mass, have been well trained, and work with marketers who've properly stacked value and established proximity, but you still can't win, you're either not trying hard enough, you have a bad leader, or you're in the wrong profession. Sales is the most noble profession in business, but remember this: "second place is the first loser." Make us proud.

Educate (Proximity and Antigravity)

It's gratifying that the world finally caught up to what we salespeople have known for a long time. In the sales profession, it's common knowledge that the seller's viewpoint is the fifth most important aspect of influence. Put another way, nobody gives a shit what salespeople say. Buyers want insight, not information.

In 2016, I spoke at a cybersecurity conference in Singapore. To start my presentation, I informed the audience that the content they were about to see had never been seen before; that what I was about to share could only be learned by those in the room at that moment. My topic was my groundbreaking analysis of a crushing ransomware attack. All phones went down, all eyes went up to the stage. I was sharing insight, not just information.

My guidance on educate, the fourth and final element of the SAVE framework, is pretty simple.

1. **Educate with insight, not information**. Insight cultivates feelings of emotional superiority. Information that's readily available does not move the needle.

2. **Remove barriers**. Knowledge is power. Make your insightful content readily available throughout the customer journey. Share your best "aha" and "oh shit" insights far and wide. Occasionally, you may choose to restrict access to insight in exchange for the customer's contact information (e.g., "subscribe to our free newsletter to read this special report"). That's a fair trade-off in my opinion, but don't overdo it.

3. **Content mapping strategy.** Marketing people are usually pretty good at writing content customers want to consume. Beyond writing skill, the key to an effective content strategy is mapping. Refer back to the eight-category mapping exercise in the solution section. Note the categories where you believe your offer can make the customer feel superior. Explain why with insights that drive home the reason why. For the categories where you're OK with being satisfactory, you can probably get away with sharing information without much insight using functional descriptions.

4. **Remember that less is more.** In the Moonshot section, you learned about the value trap called grid jumping. Your product maximizes your website's loading speed, changes your oil, and regrows your hair. Oh, and it's for your parents, the kids, and the dog at home. Buy one, get one free. Don't try to be everything to everyone. As you educate, put most of your chips on the one or two outcomes that represent the preponderance of your value stack and stick to the stack!

5. **Strive to lower the cost of customer thinking.** This is straight from the week I spent studying business marketing strategy at Kellogg. This means succinctly connecting your inner core to what's likely to be the most valuable outcome to the customer. That's the idea behind your brand promise statement, and it needs to be reinforced throughout your strategy to educate the marketplace.

6. **Whatever you do, don't forget antigravity.** Remember to use the phrase "unlike alternatives" as you educate customers. Invest in antigravity strategies so you can deliver insight on competitors, not just information. This is badly overlooked at most companies. Do make that mistake, or you are wasting gravity.

Integrated Marketing

My first experience running a big marketing team was at Trend Micro, where almost one hundred people reported to me, including product managers, product marketers, analyst relations, demand generation specialists, field marketers, and interns. Marketing people are great. They're smart, energetic, hardworking, and creative. There's just one problem: there aren't enough Shot Callers in marketing. And integrated marketing is an approach I'm recommending to help us get there.

The term *integrated marketing* is often used in conjunction with *integrated CMO*. Both refer to the same idea. A marketing function or marketing leader who aligns with the business at every phase is deemed to be "integrated." It's really no different from saying the marketing team is Shot Calling. Integrated marketers understand the need to call their shots because they are ultimately looking to create business outcomes, not just execute on activity.

I've known some really great integrated marketing leaders in my career. They all behaved like Shot Callers in their marketing roles. They were never afraid to set strong revenue outcomes for products they worked on or marketed, and they were adept at working cross-functionally to get the desired result. As a result, these individuals delivered big achievements and reached C-level status as business operators, not just as marketers.

What I learned from these people is that marketing is a means to a business end. Most other marketers I worked with saw their job as getting a million tasks done. It's true that marketing requires more juggling than any other role. It's also at the intersection of every other business function, which creates tremendous potential for people. So just as these individuals emerged from marketing roles into big-time business roles through integrated marketing, so can you by becoming a Shot Caller!

Here's my guidance for becoming a Shot Caller through integrated marketing:

1. **Align Kill Shot key performance indicators to the Moonshot**. Document them in your SAVE plan. It's virtually impossible to execute a strategy without the marketing team and its leader being committed.

2. **Take names, get results.** Ideas are like your children; they become orphans if you don't give them a name. That's what I tell everyone who asks me how to advance their career. It's especially true for marketing staff, who rarely get credit for their results. Every program, campaign, initiative, or activity should have a name and a targeted result that gets reported. That's how you can amass the gravity of your results into your personal brand instead of the myriad participants who are happy to accept the additional gravity of a good outcome. Remember, success has a thousand fathers, and failure is an orphan.

3. **Create a marketing calendar.** When I took over as general manager at Trend Micro, I inherited a team of six hundred, which included about five hundred engineers and about a hundred marketers. The reason I was put in the job was to bring predictability to the business. Basically, I was put there to create Shot Callers, even though I wouldn't have said it that way at the time. The

team had many talented people, but something was missing. We were not delivering something people could rely on. Sometimes the products did not have enough marketing support. Sometimes the documentation wasn't any good. Sometimes the messaging wasn't insightful. There were a million little things that had to be accounted for. So I created something we called the "Big Board." Think of it as a calendar with color-coded columns and rows. We listed every campaign, program, launch, and event on this spreadsheet; assigned each task a level one, two, or three priority, with one being drop-everything-else-do-this-now; and published the calendar for everyone to see. We also included the results we expected from each activity with dates for when each activity needed to be executed and at what priority level on a global basis. This created instant gravity for my team and, most importantly, forced everyone to call their shots, not just juggle a million balls. Shot calling is a system for success. One of the best ways to know it works is to watch it work. At Trend Micro, we went from herding cats and scrambling to track everything to having a bulletproof system to get all the work done right. The result was eighteen tier 1, all-hands-on-deck launches over a three-year period—a record to this day—all executed without a hitch. The term *Big Board* also entered the lexicon of the company. Everyone knew what it meant. There are many variants on how to execute a marketing calendar. Most are good enough. The key is to turn one into a system for how work gets done. The Big Board was mine. It's fine if yours gets called something else, just make sure you have one.

4. **Theme your campaigns**. Shot Callers don't waste time or money marketing shit no one cares about. What is your offer's inner core? What outcomes do customers value most? How do those outcomes make them feel? How are they worth it? Your solution packaging grid gives you eight job outcome categories to theme around. Your value is contained in ones where you can deliv-

er superior emotional outcomes. That's where your campaign themes should focus. At Trend Micro, we had a solution that could find cyber threats in your network so you could minimize the likelihood of a data breach. We could deliver superior outcomes, especially in helping customers locate and confirm their fear that they had been hacked. So our marketing team created a campaign theme called "Think Again." We challenged the marketplace with the following statement: "If you think you haven't been breached, think again." The call to action to customers was to run a test with our solution to prove it to them. This campaign ran successfully for months because it was properly themed to our strength. That's what all good campaigns should do.

5. **Growth hack while Shot Calling**. At the time of this writing, "growth marketing" is a new term generally used to describe any effort to drive revenue through digital channels. It's sometimes referred to as "growth hacking" for that reason. I've worked with several growth hackers with mixed results. The best part of any growth strategy is it's a fast, data-centric way to drive performance, often at low cost. The problem is, "if you torture the data long enough, it will confess to anything," as the saying goes. It's especially true if the growth hacker is a Kabuki Dancer. There's a massive amount of material on this subject, and the science of growth marketing is closer to engineering than marketing, anyway. So we're not diving deep here on growth marketing. I'll just say this: Growth hacking is a massively powerful proximity play that can create immense gravity if done well. However, it doesn't change any of the parameters of the Three Rs Test. You are not going to magically growth hack your way to sustained success.

6. **Measure progress.** Everywhere I've worked, the more business growth slowed, the more shit we measured. Here's what I can promise you: measuring doesn't drive performance; Shot Calling drives performance. Measuring progress helps inform your

decisions and keep you on track, but that's all. The KPIs from the Whole Shot Grid are what should be measured like they're the difference between life and death. Prove you can alter gravity on those before you measure one more damn thing. Otherwise, you are merely Kabuki dancing your way to KPI hell.

THE MONEY SHOT

When I took a shot at how many sales calls I've been on over the years, I estimated over forty thousand. So let's be conservative and say twenty thousand. On top of that, I've been trained in some form of sales methodology or performance strategy just about every year of my career. I've also conducted sales training and led teams of more than a hundred sales professionals through extensive sales enablement and certification processes five times. I've done every sales job from individual contributor to chief revenue officer (CRO). I was named twice to the Chairman's top performer list—once at MCI where a hundred out fifteen thousand people were selected and again at Trend Micro where five out of thirty-five hundred employees received this recognition. I achieved President's club-level performance twelve out of fourteen years as an individual contributor, twice winning Sales Rep of the Year. I've won numerous awards as a sales leader because my teams always overperformed. Add books read, consultants hired, coursework completed, and peers learned from, and I have easily an advanced degree in sales. By any measure, I am an elite expert in the field.

I have never sold the industry-leading product in my entire career. Even with that handicap, I consistently outperformed peers, often lapping their results. The expression "whatever doesn't kill you makes you stronger," is a big part of my own inner core. Knowing I would get fired if I didn't win was my constant companion. I simply couldn't succeed if I didn't figure out what worked and why.

Sales is a brutal yet beautiful profession that way. An old boss of mine used to run across the room when she saw me to give me a hug. As long as my numbers were good. When they were off, she wouldn't even look at me. All sales professionals know exactly what I'm talking about. Our profession has a "what have you done for me lately?" culture. "Sell or die" is the sword constantly above our heads. Nobody cares. Not friends, co-workers, bosses, investors, board members. Nobody. Think I'm exaggerating? The average tenure of a CRO is now nine months. That's criminal, and nobody cares. On top of that, everyone tells you, "We're all in sales." What bullshit. Unless you carry a quota, you're not in sales. I once told the board of a company I led sales at, "I've forgotten more about sales than you'll ever know," which is a 100 percent true statement. They got offended, and I probably shouldn't have said it, but tough shit.

I'm grateful for all the scar tissue I carry. It gave me skin thick enough to survive and prosper in sales for over thirty years. Sales taught me what works in business and what doesn't. Most of all, it forced me to become a Shot Caller. Not because I wanted to. Because I had to.

Your turn.

Unless you're selling a solution with so much mass customers just buy it, it's Money Shot or die. Let's start.

Success Is a Planned Event

One of the best speakers I've ever heard is Lou Holtz, the former Notre Dame football coach. He gave a keynote while I was at MCI. During the speech, he asked, "How do you think Sir Edmund Hillary became the first person to climb Mount Everest? Do you think he had a plan? Or did he just go out for a walk one day and suddenly discovered he was on the top?"

The audience laughed. I was struck by the irony. It felt like most MCI leadership was "out for a walk." I hadn't yet heard the term *Kabuki dancing*, but going out for a walk and Kabuki dancing are two sides of the same coin. Success can be planned, but it's not the plan that causes the success. You need a *system* for success. That's Shot Calling.

Like the Kill Shot builds on the Moonshot, the Money Shot expands on both. The elements of the Shot-Calling System work together. Your vision and mission are clear. Your value is stacked. Your strategy moves are mapped out. Your brand promise and value stack proposition are done, and your solution is packaged. Now let's go sell something!

Not so fast. It took me a long time to realize that success planning means more than setting a goal. I grew up with old-school ideas like "fog the mirror," a technique to remind yourself your income goal for the year. Each morning after your shower, use your finger to draw your desired income on the condensation-fogged mirror. At one point, $100,000 seemed like all the money in the world. The theory behind this approach is that planting that goal in your mind every morning compels you to behave in ways likely to make you realize the goal.

Not a bad idea, but there's a problem. Goals aren't enough. You need a system for success. Systems beat goals. That's why every territory, region, country, or company I've joined saw sales increase while I was there and decrease after I left. It's not because they couldn't figure out how to set goals, it's because they either didn't have a success system or have the right person driving the system.

Just like every CMO should desire to be an integrated executive who masters all five shots, so should you want to be an integrated sales professional. I don't care if you're an inside rep (I was for the first two years of my career), a field rep, channel rep, national rep, global rep, sales manager, director, VP, EVP, or Chief Revenue Officer. You must become integrated—learn all five shots—if you're to become a Shot Caller.

Think Backward

Start at the end. That's what I learned through years as an individual contributor and leader. The best way to predict what's possible is to model all outcomes from worst to best. I often tell my teams and reps to "set the goalposts." This means establishing a revenue performance range with revenue right in the middle as the most likely result. If your performance isn't more or less in the middle, you suck at predicting the edges. Accurate predictions—true Shot Calling—makes you a sales master. If you miss wide on either side of the center, you need to deconstruct the reasons why using Shot Calling and figure out why you got it wrong.

I'm amazed at how many businesses can't even perform to their worst-case model. That's business malpractice, plain and simple. Don't ever accept some Kabuki Dancer telling you it's OK if salespeople miss their targets. That's a destructive lie. As a sales leader, I've often been asked, "What percentage of your sales team do you expect to beat their plan?" My answer is always, "All of them." Now, that never happens for reasons you already understand, but why would I ever accept anyone underperforming? Don't. Shot Callers know how to get everyone productive.

Another misbelief is that "stretch" targets motivate sales professionals. I was once in a meeting with the executive team to kick off our sales planning process. The CEO-Founder took a rubber band out of his pocket.

"Watch this." He pulled the rubber band back almost to its breaking point, then released it. We all watched it fly across the room. He retrieved the rubber band and held it up. "See? Tension creates energy. If we want to go far, we must stretch ourselves."

That was his way of saying he was about to set sales quotas too high. I didn't push back. I simply asked for the rubber band, pulled it back until it broke and dropped to the floor. It didn't fly anywhere.

"See? Too much tension kills performance."

My point is just as true now as it was then. Healthy tension is fine. Unhealthy tension is antigravity inside your own organization. That's never helpful. Never. Insistence that salespeople set unreasonable targets often comes from the top—CEOs, founders, investors, board members. Usually, these people have never carried a sales quota in their lives. Obviously, they are successful in their own right. Most are extremely driven, especially around "mission." Remember the definition? A mission is the committed endeavor, the thing you are so committed to that you will either succeed or die trying.

Well, that's what leaders want, the "die trying" part. Pushing salespeople sounds good. Everyone works until no stone is unturned and there are no more hours in the day. Collapsing over the finish as you just manage to hit your targets. That's what winning feels like, right? Nope. That's just powerful people indulging their belief system. Sure, effort matters. I worked my ass off, but I never benefited from unrealistic expectations, and I never ran teams that way. Anyone who pitches the idea that fear drives performance is selling you a lie. I challenge anyone who believes that: Let's both take the same title, same product, and territories of equal opportunity, and let's bet $1 million on who sells the most after one year. I dare you to take me up on this. I can't imagine a VC quitting that job, going into sales, and losing a million bucks to me, though. I wish someone would. My points are:

- Unrealistic or inaccurate targets cause weakness, not strength.
- Healthy tension increases performance. Fear as an indulgence reduces gravity and hurts performance.
- Shot Callers set their goalposts and deliver accurate high performance. If they miss, they explore all five shots, fix the why—not the who—and do better next time.
- You need a plan, but Shot Calling leads to wins, not the planning. I'm living proof. Bet me if you don't believe me. I dare you.

Productivity Modeling

Setting the goalposts starts with a productivity model like the one I'm about to show you. I designed the spreadsheet and visualizations at Emailage with Operations VP and "Guardian of the Galaxy" Anthony

Enrico. The point of any modeling exercise is to make the best prediction you can. You're looking into a crystal ball to forecast yield.

If I do X, how much performance will I get from Y?

For years, I've said that "What I am getting for my money?" is the easiest question to ask and hardest to answer. Anthony and I contemplated starting a company that would focus on just that question. We even came up with a name—"Yieldly." Its mission was to help people build the best version of their crystal ball.

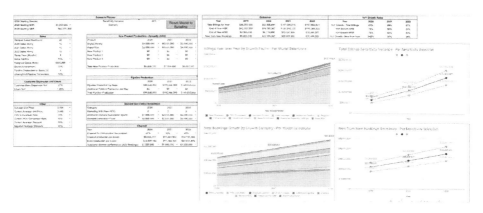

Figure 3.1 Sample productivity model.

Just like the SAVE framework in the Kill Shot maps to business gravity, any modeling exercise you complete reflects your Whole Shot Grid in three ways. Here's how.

1. **Mass**: Model any solutions or products that have mass. Assume you or your people are selling your current offers. It is *essential* that whoever insisted the product gets built also help predict its revenue impact. This goes back to my Kill Shot guidance on solution-level forecasting. The only way anyone learns how to do this is to actually do it, so do not skip this step. You can also model based on productivity. I'm used to having a bunch of salespeople delivering revenue, so I almost always start with modeling productivity per head using projected sales quotas.

If you add more solutions into the mix, model those separately using the "new product" section. Account for any new salesperson's "ramp time" as well. Will it take them three months to reach full production or nine? How much attrition across sales teams do you anticipate? What percentage is likely to reach full production? Basically, model all the strategies intended to add mass.

2. **Proximity**: In the productivity model, proximity is anything that represents an additional investment to get closer to customers. The spreadsheet makes this easy, so don't worry too much about it. "Current-level" investments, often referred to as "run rate," should already be baked in, so just focus on additional investment as you build your model. These could include (but are not limited to) new investments in demand generation, events, channel development, search engine optimization, content marketing, or antigravity maneuvers. These variables have an impact you can model either as some amount of absolute gain ("this event will generate X dollars of pipeline and revenue") or as a yield percentage increase. For example, improving lead quality may result in X percent lead conversion improvement or X percent pilot or trial conversion increases. Again, the spreadsheet takes care of this as long as the data you input is accurate.

3. **Orbit**: This includes any variable that affects your unit economics. Normally, I don't model for the cost side of the business, but you can include that, too, if necessary. Otherwise, orbit largely refers to investments that impact pricing or discounting. Sales training is an investment designed to improve your team's ability to pass the Three Rs Test. Such investments can be modeled for performance gains in average sale price or average discount percentage. Again, the model accounts for these, so do your best to be accurate.

When I was at Malwarebytes, I deployed an artificial intelligence tool called Clari. This is the future of modeling, but as awesome as the technology is, it has limits we can learn from. "Garbage in, garbage out" is still the forecasting rule. Getting good at this takes practice, even for AI engines like Clari. It was not that accurate for the first two quarters of use, and then it became freakishly accurate. Even AI has a ramp!

My rule of thumb is that Shot Callers can model +/- 10 percent on either side of a business outcome (the goal posts). At Trend Micro, I modeled within $100,000 of a $165 million plan because I knew the business and called my shots. With all the tools available, you should never be outside that 10 percent range. Frankly, 10 percent is too high, but I'm being generous. If you're outside that range, you're not Shot Calling, you're just guessing . . . also known as Kabuki dancing.

Money Mapping

What's the most important item to have if you're going on a treasure hunt? A treasure map! What's the second most important thing? To know how much treasure is still there! I've been trying to make a treasure map and calculate the available loot for the last three decades. Until now, it's been impossible. I've used every resource known to exist, like www.Discover.org, Rainking, Hoovers, Gartner, and feedback from my sales teams, to map out the "total addressable market" for the broadest of all industries, cybersecurity. It's global and ubiquitous because everyone from individual consumers to the largest enterprises and national governments needs cybersecurity. All I've ever wanted to know is how many people and organizations (i.e., potential customers) exist in any given geography and how much money they have to spend on my offer. Easy to ask, almost impossible to know for certain.

Even so, it's possible to estimate with some sense of accuracy similar to how you use productivity modeling to predict performance between the +/- 10 percent goal posts. Any money map is better than none. The data you need to make yours includes:

- Total number of targets (companies or consumers)

- A breakdown of how many are already customers and how many are not
- For your nonbuyers, total spending potential (available spend, not total budget)

There is no excuse for not having at least a basic money map, even if you are an individual contributor. Shot Callers want more than that, though. At Emailage, we started to make the first viable money map I'd ever seen. LexisNexis bought us before we could finish, but I have no doubt we would have. Our great breakthrough came when we bought Tableau, a data visualization software. We used the tool to create a map of each region in the world and display our sales coverage as a series of circles indicating which person covered which geography. Tableau allowed us to zoom in on each area of coverage to see the underlying data, including:

- The accounts in the geography and whether they were new or existing customers
- The available spend for each account
- The salesperson's performance versus their quota to indicate how well they were doing finding and extracting the treasure (this indicated the health of each territory)

Here's the money map we made at Emailage. Thank Bernado Alves, another Guardian of the Galaxy and our resident Tableau expert.

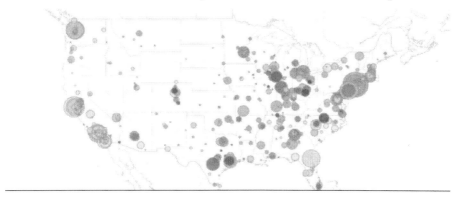

Figure 3.2 Sample money map: Emailage.

I cannot emphasize enough how important money mapping is if you want to be a Shot Caller. For leaders, it's the holy grail of performance management. Maps are damn hard to make, but they're worth it. A money map is where you find the truth. Salespeople armed with an accurate money map and backed by a supportive manager are unstoppable.

Revenue Delivery Platform

Also known as an execution workflow, a revenue delivery platform is a detailed description of who does what and when during the customer life cycle. The four platform components I've used at every company at which I've led sales are:

1. A content strategy that maps to the SAVE plan

2. A workflow strategy that maps to the customer life cycle from "cradle to grave"

3. A handoff strategy indicating which functions live in sales and which live in marketing

4. A measurement strategy for gauging performance and making adjustments

I don't want to make revenue delivery platform setup seem simple. It's not. But it's also not rocket science. Most revenue delivery platforms include outbound and inbound content strategy, the customer lifecycle, and the sales funnel. Together, these pieces answer the questions, where and how are we going to acquire customers?

Being a Shot Caller demands that you accept the truth. These revenue delivery platforms don't deliver the revenue. Shot Callers do. Do not mistake "operationalizing" for Shot Calling. You need both. But if your Moonshot lacks gravity, your Kill Shot and Money Shot are both off. In that case, you're wasting time operationalizing your revenue delivery platform. It's like practicing a bad golf swing. Sure, you'll get better to a point, but beyond that, you are ingraining weakness. Be a

Shot Caller. In all my years in sales, I've never seen anything work sustainably except Shot Calling. I've also never seen the best revenue delivery platforms improve performance more than 10 percent, and even that was temporary. Once the gain is realized, that's all the blood you get from that stone.

Symbolize Winning

Success is a poor teacher and a false god. Winning teaches you the wrong lessons about why you won. I'm not saying each win has no takeaways. They do. But "success has a thousand fathers" because everyone wants credit. Every win report I've ever written or read says the same thing. *We won because the customer valued our solution for these reasons and our team for these reasons, so I'd like to thank . . .*

"Loss reports" are all the same too. *We lost because of competition, features, price, and the dreaded "no decision."* No one ever admits they lost because they screwed up the sale. If a customer didn't buy, something went wrong—but what?

This section of the Money Shot is about the big stuff you have to get right to win in sales. There is a mountain of material already published on sales methodologies, persuasion, the psychology of closing techniques, qualifying techniques, and so on. I've taken dozens of training courses and read many books on all of them. Most are pretty good. You need to be reasonably proficient at all of it if you're going to be a good salesperson. Put skin in the game and learn them on your own. After all, this book is about creating Shot Callers, not teaching sales methodologies, so we will focus on the fundamentals of winning, the "first principles" of the sales profession. I'm an expert on this subject, and I have many friends who are as well. The ideas you're about to read represent the consensus among the best of the best. Embrace our conclusions, and you'll become a Money Shot Caller who consistently wins for the rest of your career.

Sales is the most noble business profession, but it's also the most brutal. I learned long ago that "second place is the first loser" in sales. You can put in all the work but end up heartbroken. I'm not saying you'll win every deal, but I *can* teach how to give yourself the best chance to win every deal. Now let's sell something!

Sales Is a Symbols Game

This is the true first principle of selling. Yes, I changed the saying "sales is a numbers game," to "a symbols game," and you'll understand why shortly. I feel so strongly about this principle that I flat-out tell anyone who disagrees, *"You are not one of us . . . you will not be on one of my teams . . . you don't know shit about sales . . . and you will never be a Shot Caller."* I make no apologies for being harsh. I've learned over thirty-five years of selling and going on twenty-thousand sales calls that "sales is a symbols game" is the absolute truth.

Picture a funnel with a number sign (#) at the top, a percent sign (%) in the middle, and a dollar sign ($) at the bottom. These are the symbols of sales.

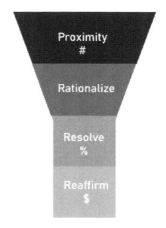

Figure 3.3 The symbols of sales.

This funnel depicts the three stages of the sales process. The beauty is its mathematical simplicity. Once you know your numbers, you can decide how you want to play your "symbols game." Shot Callers notice the relationship between the gravity moves and this funnel. When you bring an offer with mass to the market, executing your proximity moves aligns to the top of the funnel (#). Rationalizing and resolving occur through the sales process, but always start with rationalizing value before you start trying to influence how the customer feels about your offer. The bottom of the funnel is where the winning occurs. That's where you balance the forces necessary to win by adjusting economic value as necessary. I typically bet most on the top of the funnel, the # symbol. I'll explain why later, but let's break each down so you can decide where your efforts are best spent.

Know Your Number (#)

The top of funnel is easy to measure in terms of:

1. Number of opportunities in the funnel

2. Frequency and velocity of opportunities entering and exiting the funnel

3. Value of opportunities in the funnel (weighted and unweighted)

4. Product composition of opportunities in the funnel (Are you selling your full portfolio?)

5. Lead or influence source of opportunities in the funnel

I hope this stage seems straightforward, because it is. Everything else being equal, if you have enough opportunities of the right size across your full spectrum of products sourced or influenced from the proper channels, you will win—if your numbers bear out. No rocket science here. A simple productivity model can calculate the production necessary to overperform on those five variables.

By now, you've probably guessed why I bet on the top of the funnel.

You can affect it the most through hard work. I was never blessed in my career to sell for a market leader or to get hot leads handed to me. I had no choices besides sell or die, so I learned to grind. I'll bet on a grinder every time. My buddy Brian Harmon gets props; he taught me the value of grinding. To this day, I consider him the only sales rep who might be able to beat me if we went head-to-head. Good luck.

Young reps I hire don't believe me when I tell them this story. When Brian and I worked at MCI, our sales manager put all twelve sales reps' names on a whiteboard and charted our funnel performance along the same lines I described earlier in the number breakdown. Every six weeks, our manager put the lowest performer on a performance improvement plan (PIP). That person's plan required one thing: get off the bottom within the next six-week period, or pack up your shit and go home because you're fired. Our manager was an asshole, but if you were on his team, you learned how to grind in a hurry. Sell or die.

I'll leave you with one more story before we proceed to the next stage. Before CRM systems took forecasting digital, charting and predicting sales performance was often done in a common area on a chalkboard or whiteboard like at MCI. Imagine your name on a board with your prospects listed by sales stage with close probability and deal value. All out in the open. Today's CRMs display all that and more, but there was something special about forcing salespeople to write down our numbers so our co-workers and managers could stare at them constantly. You felt totally naked. If your numbers were shitty, you were. That feeling taught us a lesson—the people who took care of business at the top of their funnel never had a problem. The people who couldn't get their shit together at "stage one" eventually had a problem.

I've outsold and outlasted just about everyone I've ever worked with in sales. After Emailage, I decided to retire from the profession because I did really well—and because I'd rather create Shot Callers than keep selling. If I ever return to an operating role, I'll win again. As sure as God made little green apples, I'll take care of the top of the funnel. So should you.

Know Your Percent (%)

If # symbolizes effort—the grind-it-out, make-it-happen attitude you need to build a healthy funnel—the % and $ symbolize your ability to win those deals. One of my all-time favorite basketball players, Magic Johnson, refers to the last five minutes of a game as "winning time." That's what happens with % and $: winning or losing. You've executed your numbers game and (I hope) have a full funnel. To maximize your chance of winning, you must pass the Three *R*s Test.

1. Rationalize functional value.

2. Resolve your customers' need to feel superior or satisfied with your solution.

3. Reaffirm economic value.

Every time I've won a deal, I passed the Three *R*s Test. Every time I've lost, I failed the test. The logical question is, "OK, asshole, how do salespeople pass the Three *R*s Test?" That's the right question, but remember, this book is not about teaching you sales methodology, it's about making you a Shot Caller. Don't get me wrong—I'm a huge fan of sales methodologies and have been trained (and trained people on) Target Account Selling, Miller Heiman's Strategic Selling, and the Challenger Sales Model. I've also read or studied just about everything on the subject that matters from the best sales consultancies like SiriusDecisions, CEB, and Gartner. For me, Challenger is most useful because the Challenger salesperson profile wins the most, making Challenger selling the most aligned to Shot Calling. Read *The Challenger Sale* by Brent Adamson and Matthew Dixon to improve your chances of passing the Three *R*s Test.

Honestly, it's easy to understand that if you can't rationalize your offer's functional value, you'll probably lose. The same is true for resolving emotional value. If your customer isn't "feeling it," you're going to lose. And if you can't convince them your offer is "worthy" by reaffirming economic value, you lose. Shot Callers prefer winning, so let's look at what you must account for when interacting with the customer so they're more likely to say yes. Again, this is the what, not the how. Trust me—the market will inform you soon enough if you need improvement. Basically, if you keep getting your ass kicked and failing the Three *R*s Test, you'd better change how you sell.

Two more important comments before we review the Three *R*s Test together. First, your antigravity strategy should manifest in every sales conversation. That's why my Three *R*s Test cheat sheet includes the phrase "compared to alternatives." You're not Shot Calling unless you're applying antigravity.

Second, as a sales professional, you're often at the mercy of how well your company supports your attempts to rationalize and resolve. It's shitty to send salespeople into battle if the entire business hasn't done their part on the Three *R*s Test. Unfortunately, that happens all the time. I'm afraid we're stuck with that until we create more Shot Callers in the world. When it comes to reaffirming economic value, convincing the customer your offer is worth it, that's on you. Top salespeople do this, and I'll teach you how in the next section. For now, let's look at that cheat sheet I promised. How well you rationalize functional value, resolve emotional needs, and reaffirm economic value (i.e., the quality of your pitch) are based on several variables. Here they are.

The Three *R*s Test Cheat Sheet

1. Quality of ability to rationalize functional value by:
   a. Effectively <u>communicating</u> inner core uniqueness compared to alternatives
   b. Effectively <u>demonstrating</u> inner core uniqueness compared to alternatives
   c. Quantifying the value of your solution compared to alternatives by connecting it to the "highest level of strategic intersection" (more on this shortly)

2. Quality of ability to resolve emotional needs by:

    a. Emotionally drowning your customer in the wisdom of your position to cause healthy tension (yes, this comes from *The Challenger Sale*'s Rational Drowning; more on that below)
    b. Effectively resolving that tension by extolling the virtue of your offer
    c. Emotionally disrupting the worthiness of alternatives (antigravity)
    d. Establishing the feeling your offer is legitimate through third-party endorsements

3. Quality of ability to reaffirm economic value by:

    a. Accurately identifying the highest level of strategic intersection
    b. Accurately identifying and classifying key stakeholders
    c. Effectively establishing your offer's worthiness and undermining the worthiness of alternatives throughout the sales process
    d. Winning the deal

Here's another way to think of the Three *R*s Test. The book *The Challenger Sale* popularized the term *Rational Drowning*. The authors did extensive research on why the same salespeople kept overperforming compared to their peers. A key similarity was their capacity to invade the customer's consciousness, or "rationally drown" them, during the sale process. This means making such a compelling case for an offer's functional and economic value that any doubts or reservations get "drowned out." Subsequently, the customer has been "rationally drowned" in the logic of your solution and can complete the emotional process known as "transference," which is a successful attempt to influence how customers think and feel about your offer. As a direct result, the brain shifts from interest to desire—"love at first sight."

If you've been in sales long enough, you can sense that moment instantly. It's an awesome feeling. Functional value was rationalized, emotions were resolved, and economic value was reaffirmed. You passed the test.

What if you're bombing the test? The harsh reality is that it's your or your company's fault. Shot Callers and companies that practice Shot Calling accept this reality and work their asses off until both marketing and sales can pass the test. They focus on the *why*, not the *who*, and get the job done. Kabuki Dancers blame everyone but themselves, then go create another hundred KPIs to search for answers that aren't there. Please don't do that. Go back to your Moonshot strategy and figure out what you missed. Not enough mass or antigravity? Were you unequipped to rationalize functional value once you achieved proximity? Was your value stack off? Did you underestimate opposing gravity? You will always find the answer in those questions. That's where Shot Callers look while Kabuki Dancers run around looking for someone to blame.

Know Your Money ($)

My career started in inside sales with a hardcore routine of a hundred "dials" per day and twenty-five "talks," meaning I was required to have twenty-five actual sales conversations every day. It was hard, but I did it well for two years and got promoted to field sales at age twenty-four largely on my strength as a grinder. My field sales assignment was a territory in New Jersey where I was one of seven sales reps. We each had approximately two hundred accounts to call on or prospect. *What a joke,* I thought at the time. I managed over two thousand accounts in my insides sales job.

In classic grinder fashion, I decided to play the "numbers game" to win. I quickly realized I could build a money map of my entire territory simply by calling every prospect, introducing myself, and qualifying each account. So for the first two weeks of my field sales career, I locked myself in the office and made the calls. I'll never forget the looks I got from the other reps and our manager, who were all at least fifteen years older. They'd walk by, look in, probe me on what I was up to, and wonder if I was wasting my time.

In my third week, I hit the road to visit prospects I'd profiled and made appointments with. I had no concept of the Three Rs Test, but I somehow applied it nonetheless. All I can say is I did my best to be an effective salesperson. The product wasn't that complicated, and I was betting on my grinding ability anyway. My bet paid off. I got my first order in week four. By the fifth week, I had one of the best funnels on the team. Our manager, Alberto Pascucci, took notice. At the start of week six, Alberto kicked off the weekly staff call by describing how impressed he was with "Meeler" (that's what Miller sounds like with an Italian accent). He proceeded to call everyone out for getting shown up by a twenty-four-year-old. Suddenly, I was the center of attention. The truth is, these older reps knew more about sales than I did, but I was a better grinder simply because I didn't know any different.

Alberto announced that we needed "the best of both worlds." He asked me to teach the older reps how to money map, and he asked them to teach me how to sell. It was a good move, especially for me, because the sales veterans took me under their wings. That's what got me going in the real profession of "capital S" Sales. Thirty-five years and many thousands of sales calls later, I've concluded that one thing separates winners from losers. **Winners seek and sell to the highest level of strategic intersection**.

The Highest Level of Strategic Intersection

The two true stories you're about to read are my signature wins as a salesperson who sought and sold to the highest level of strategic intersection. Before we jump in, I'm going to explain what that means through a concept called *Level 1, 2, 3 Selling*.

- Level 1 sellers can tell you what a product *is*.
- Level 2 sellers can tell you what a product *does*.
- Level 3 sellers can tell you what a product *means*.

Level 3 selling is synonymous with seeking and selling to the highest level of strategic intersection. At the end of each story, I'll distinguish between levels 1, 2, and 3 so you can appreciate the difference. You'll also understand why this separates the winners from the losers.

Faster Shirts

In the 1990s, I worked for Infonet, a spinoff from Computer Sciences Corporation (CSC), the first publicly traded software company. Infonet provided wide-area data networking services within CSC. Back then, data communications was highly regulated outside the United States. That's where Infonet played best. The funky part was Infonet's ownership structure was made up of about a dozen different foreign governments.

From my role, I sold services like frame relay (don't worry if you don't know what that is; it doesn't matter). Our inner core was the service delivery advantage that came with our foreign ownership. Our size, hardware, and network speed were all inferior to major players like MCI and AT&T. If you needed data networking service installed overseas and delivered with some local, personal attention, Infonet was a good choice because of our unique relationships with foreign telecommunications authorities.

Liz Claiborne, the women's fashion brand, was an existing customer. Several locations used our service, mostly in Asia. They wanted to upgrade their entire global network, and we were invited to participate. Infonet engineers worked closely with Liz Claiborne to design the best possible solution. Even our best didn't look good. Our network was a lot more expensive for the same service the market leaders could provide.

At a meeting in New Jersey with the Liz Claiborne technical team, someone from their business side joined. It turned out he was responsible for all overseas Liz Claiborne manufacturing. He kept asking us how quickly we could install service at a location and move a location's existing service to another facility. Pretty normal questions. His technical guys offered reassurance, insisting they had a handle on "change management" so he didn't need to worry about it.

Not so fast, skippy, I thought. There was more here than met the eye. I asked my account contact if he'd be willing to set up a meeting with me and this person. Just him, my contact, and me. He did. In that follow-up conversation, I learned that fashion isn't filled with Shot Callers either. The head of garment manufacturing explained to me how the industry works.

"We really have no idea what clothes are going to be popular going into any season. So we just manufacture a shitload of clothes we think are going to be the rage and put them in market. Once the wholesalers and retailers figure out what people are buying, we adjust our manufacturing strategy to make more of the popular garments and fewer unpopular ones. To balance our costs, we bundle the popular and unpopular garments together and force buyers to take the entire bundle. That's the only way they can get their hands on the good stuff, and it's the only way we can control our costs.

"Unfortunately, fashion is so fickle and moves so quickly that unless we can make enough of the good stuff in time to capture the market, we're screwed. We end up with nothing but a bundle of garments no one wants, our brand takes a hit, and margins collapse. Sometimes, we have to add or move a manufacturing site so quickly that any delay could cause us to literally miss the market. If some shirts are super hot, I need to make them faster."

Bingo. I'd found the highest level of strategic intersection: faster shirts. What difference did Infonet's limitations make to Liz Claiborne compared to being able to deliver faster shirts?

I responded with an antigravity move. Knowing that Indonesia was a big hub for Liz Claiborne manufacturing, I asked, "Did AT&T or MCI tell you about the telecommunications strike in Indonesia?"

"What strike? No. Explain. What strike?"

"Yeah. There's a strike in the telecom industry down there right now. It's not expected to end for months, and there's no way to get installations done without special government approval."

You should've seen the look on his face. He had no clue.

"But don't worry," I said. "Infonet can make it happen because of our special relationship with the Indonesian authorities."

After that, it wasn't even a fair fight. We won. For this win, combined with the next deal you'll read about, I earned Infonet's Sales Rep of the Year Award. Liz Claiborne didn't give a shit about the "speeds and feeds" given what was at stake: improved image, more sales, happier buyers, lower costs, more profits, and *faster shirts*.

Here's how this story breaks down into the three levels of selling.

- Level 1 seller: "Hi, Liz Claiborne. Infonet **is** a wide-area, international data networking service. Would you like to buy our service?" Answer: "No. Screw off."
- Level 2 Seller: "Hi, Liz Claiborne. Infonet **does** turnkey installations of global data networking services like frame relay, which includes hardware management, network monitoring, and twenty-four-seven technical support. Would you like to buy?" Answer: "Maybe. But only if you invest tons of time and energy trying to convince me why I would pay more for inferior service, only to then tell you 'No, screw off.'"
- Level 3 Seller: "Hi, Liz Claiborne. Infonet service **means** you can improve your image and enjoy more sales, happier buyers, lower costs, more profits, and *faster shirts*. Would you like to buy?" Answer: "Hell yes! Where do I sign?"

Not on My Watch

The same year I won the Liz Claiborne deal, I was pursuing Dow Jones, publisher of the *Wall Street Journal*. Dow Jones had designed a new application called CopyFlow, which allowed for reporters to file stories from around the world and interact with their editors to make changes and get approval to print. It was a lot like Google Docs but without the internet. All documents needed to travel over a private, wide-area data network. That's where Infonet came in.

This sales process wasn't that different from Liz Claiborne. The Dow Jones technical team assembled the vendors they were interested in, and once again, Infonet had more weaknesses than strengths. Our competition was bigger, their networks faster, and ours more expensive. But they didn't have any Level 3 sellers.

The Dow Jones technical team estimated how much bandwidth the CopyFlow application needed and informed the vendors to price to that specification. It seemed like they were asking for way more bandwidth than they needed, but they honestly didn't know. Nowadays, it's easy to calculate how much bandwidth you need to move data over a private network, but back then it wasn't.

Our big competitors happily ran off and priced their solutions accordingly. I didn't. Instead, I asked if I could use a device called a LanAlyzer to study their network's transmission flow and determine how much bandwidth Dow Jones needed. They were more than happy to accommodate my request. It turned out my suspicion was correct—they needed only a fraction of what was requested.

I couldn't just tell Dow Jones, "Hey, dumbasses. This application only requires one-tenth the bandwidth you spec'd for." They'd just tell the other vendors, and I'd lose the power of my discovery. Then an interesting thing happened. Dow Jones called a meeting to review our proposal. This time, I asked that the team responsible for publishing the international *Wall Street Journal* attend. This was the same team who designed CopyFlow. I was hoping this would be my chance to find the highest level of strategic intersection. It was.

The Dow Jones executive responsible for publishing was not technically inclined, but throughout the meeting, he seemed obsessed with service availability. He wanted to know what happened in the event of a war or natural disaster. He literally asked, "What happens to the network if a nuke goes off?"

Who gives a shit about your data if a nuke goes off, I thought but kept it to myself. He was persistent in ways that seemed unusual for a publishing executive, so I asked, "Why are you so interested in service availability in times of crisis?"

His answer unlocked everything.

"Do you know how many times the international edition of the *Wall Street Journal* failed to publish during World War II?"

"No idea," I replied.

"Zero. In its entire history, do you know how many times the international edition of the *Wall Street Journal* has ever failed to publish?"

"I have no idea."

"Zero. And it's not going to happen now," he added. "Not on my watch."

Bingo. I'd found the highest level of strategic intersection. This executive didn't give a shit about speeds and feeds. He didn't even care about service availability. He just wanted to partner with a company that had their back through thick and thin, through a damn war if necessary.

After the executive's "not on my watch" comment, I turned to their networking team and said, "Infonet can build a network that is fully redundant, including backup routers at every location. Of course, the hard part is going to be the backup procedures. This equipment needs to be tested every ninety days. On top of that, coordinating all the people who need to be involved around the world to have confidence that the backup strategy will work in case the shit hits the fan. Infonet's relationships around the world can be leveraged to build a complete backup process you can depend on." Then I threw in some antigravity. "I don't believe other vendors like MCI and AT&T have the kind of relationships in place that you could depend on, do they?"

I knew the answer already. No way MCI or AT&T could pull this off, but I made them admit it in the meeting. This was quickly becoming another unfair fight, so I put the nail in the coffin.

"Did MCI or AT&T tell you their pricing is for a network that's got ten times more bandwidth than you need?"

"How's that?" the executive asked.

I explained how my sales engineer and I used a LanAlyzer to determine that CopyFlow required one-tenth the bandwidth they suspected.

"Didn't MCI or AT&T tell you this?" To finish them off, I said, "We cut the bandwidth in half in our proposal. It's still five times more than you need, which allows for growth, but we can fully cover the costs of a backup strategy with the savings on bandwidth. With Infonet, Copy-Flow will perform like a charm, and you get the security of knowing that publishing the international edition of the *Wall Street Journal* will not fail because of the network. *Not on your watch*."

We won a seven-year, multimillion-dollar deal by selling to the highest level of strategic intersection. Level 1 and 2 selling would not have gotten the job done. A "no, screw off" response was inevitable if I hadn't sold at Level 3. This deal put me over the top for Sales Rep of the Year. As a footnote, Dow Jones published news of the Infonet deal in the *Wall Street Journal*.

I could tell story after story like these. I hope you could too. I didn't know shit about fashion or publishing, but I still found the highest level of strategic intersection. I was simply persistent and a bit pushy. Frankly, that's the essence of Challenger Sales, which is why I like that framework best. Challenger reps understand Level 3 selling, but anyone can learn. Force yourself to do so, because that's what separates winning from losing and Shot Calling from Kabuki dancing.

Selling to the highest level of strategic intersection gives you two other important advantages. First, it "auto-qualifies" any account. It's damn near impossible to get into a strategic discussion without the customer expressing their budget, internal influence and ability to buy, need for the product, and purchase timeline (BANT); their metrics, economic buying decision criteria, decision process, identified pain, and their champion (MEDDIC); or whatever other qualifying method you prefer. Prospect qualification happens automatically once you make it clear you're not screwing around with Level 1 and 2 engagements.

The second big advantage Level 3 selling provides is rallying all constituents to your cause. Level 1 and 2 sellers have to contend with influencers, champions, decision makers, blockers, gatekeepers, "Seymours" (people who always want to "see more"), and every other stakeholder in the buying process.

Once you find the highest level of strategic intersection, everybody jumps on your bandwagon. Do you think anyone on Liz Claiborne's networking team got pissed at me for finding the highest level of strategic intersection? Of course not. In fact, it was the opposite. I made them look good, so they instantly became *my* champion. The same thing happened at Dow Jones, and the same thing will happen in your sales career if you seek and find the highest level of strategic intersection.

Money Shot Traps

In 2016, I attended a Silicon Valley Gartner event on marketing and sales. The lead speaker had spent most of her career in sales but pivoted to marketing. She started her session by asking the audience of 135 to raise our hands if we were in sales. My and two other attendees' hands went up. When she said to raise our hands if we were in marketing, the other 132 hands went up.

"OK, marketers. Keep your hand up if you have talked to a customer in the last two weeks," she said. After an awkward moment of silence, most hands went sheepishly down . . . I looked around the room. Three hands were still up, and mine was one of them.

"You should all be embarrassed," she said. "How the hell can you reflect the voice of the customer in your marketing if you don't talk to the damn customer?"

I seriously don't remember a single marketing tip or sales tactic from that event, but I'll never forget what I learned. As much as marketers' hearts are in the right place, they're not experts in what the customer wants or needs. They don't do the proper market research before building a product. They don't do product-level forecasts. Shit, they don't even talk to the damn customer. And they certainly are not experts in sales unless they've been in sales.

That's why the traps you're about to read about are for salespeople and sales leaders to understand what you're up against in their careers. Why do CROs have an average tenure of only nine months, with sales reps not far behind? A company with eighteen sales reps fires one every month one average. Why? Are we too stupid to do these jobs? Too lazy?

Come on. The answer is obvious, and it's why I wrote this damn book. I've sold and I've managed salespeople my entire life, and I can tell you that salespeople are not the problem. Low mass, poor proximity, incorrect value stacking, poor packaging, failed innovations, and unrealistic expectations create the environment that allows Kabuki Dancers to throw salespeople under the bus. It needs to stop. That's why my committed endeavor is to create Shot Callers and assassinate Kabuki Dancers. I do hope you'll join me on that mission. We need Shot Callers at every level in every job. We need everyone's help fixing the damage done to this profession. Until then, I want everyone in sales to prepare for these traps so you can defend yourself.

We're All in Sales, Yay!

How many times have you heard this line? For me, dozens. I can't remember a company where sooner or later some Kabuki Dancer doesn't proclaim, "We're all in sales!" Funny how you never hear anyone proclaim, "We're all in engineering," or "We're all in HR," or finance, marketing, legal, or any other damn department. If you don't carry a quota, you're not in sales.

I know that sounds harsh, but there's a dangerous side effect to this "we're all in sales" attitude. It undermines Shot Calling. Once you develop a belief that this casual, dumb attitude about the sales profession is acceptable, you also make it acceptable to underperform. As if problems like low mass, poor proximity, incorrect value stacking, poor packaging, failed innovations, and unrealistic expectations can be overcome with better selling. Bullshit. Sales needs the rest of the company focused on their shots. I promise you—I and every other sales professional on planet Earth will help. We will give you access to customers, make the introductions, set up the meetings, get you that data you need—whatever it takes to make you a better Shot Caller. Meanwhile, please, for the love of God, stop insulting the people who've devoted their entire lives to this profession. Do your job and let us do ours.

Glow It Right

Before I joined Trend Micro, I spent two years at a company called Voxeo. Don't worry about what they did. What matters is that's where I met Lane Bess, who eventually brought me into Trend Micro and later ZScaler. He tried to bring me into Palo Alto Networks, and I stupidly turned him down. Twice. Lane joined Voxeo as head of sales and brought me in to run the US sales team. To call that place a shitshow is an insult to shitshows. That's how badly the company was failing at all five shots. Like a lot of startups, Voxeo simply didn't have enough mass. In reality, it had almost none.

In classic Kabuki-dancing fashion, the CEO fired Lane and brought in two sales leaders from another company, one as VP and the other as a consultant. I have no hesitation in saying that the employee was a train wreck and the consultant wasn't much better. They both spent time at a hosting company during the dot-com era when the market was on fire. There was zero opposing gravity, and anyone with a decent offer was destined to succeed, and they did. I'm not saying these guys didn't work hard, but zero opposing gravity environments are the Kabuki Dancers' nursery. These guys learned all the wrong lessons about what does and doesn't work because everything worked. The VP kept telling stories about how sales should "feel," how it "wasn't about the data, it was about the energy." Shit, at one point, the consultant told me, "Tom, it's not about whether the sky is blue or purple, you need to make the sky whatever color we need." To this day, I don't know what the hell he was talking about.

Six months later, the CEO and 90 percent of her employees were fired. The founders kept me on as the only salesperson.

"Any time anything good happens, the story includes your name," one cofounder said.

I told them I'd stay under one condition: I could tell the VP to his face he was fired. They were more than happy to let me. That was my first Kabuki Dancer assassination.

My good friend Mark Patton and I spent hours comparing notes on Shot Calling. We didn't call it that, but Mark and I were always aligned on what worked. Mark introduced me to the phrase "glow it right" one day as he talked about how he'd seen companies fail to scale. Instead of learning Shot Calling, they relied on the good old days when everything "just worked," when the collective "energy," "noise level," "buzz," and Jedi mind tricks seemed to magically work. As if some collective effort to "glow it right" was more important than doing it right. Shot Callers do it right; Kabuki Dancers try to glow it right. Don't tolerate this magic thinking, or it will haunt you long after you're fired.

Sales Is Hard Enough

Don't ever make it harder. I made that promise to myself about twelve years into my career. I swore to the sales gods that if I was ever promoted to manager, I would honor the pledge that because sales was already hard, I would never make it harder for my team than it already is. To this day, I've kept that promise for reasons that will make sense once you read the Three-Point Shot.

For now, I'll share the experience that made me realize why I made that promise. I was in my early thirties and working at MCI. The company was going through an insane growth phase, including massive industry consolidation through acquisition. We'd gone from eight thousand to eighty thousand people in a five-year period. The number of people coming and going, hired and fired, was nuts. When my boss got fired, I had no clue what to do. I'd always gotten along with my managers, was a "team player," followed orders, and towed the line. All that happy horseshit. It seemed weird to suddenly have no boss, so I wandered the organization looking for guidance or affirmation. I wanted someone to tell me I was doing the right thing, but all I kept hearing was, "Just sell, and the rest will take care of itself," so that's what I did.

Working boss free felt like a giant weight lifted off my shoulders. No more check-ins, deal reviews, ride-alongs, forecast calls, weekly meetings, audits, unwanted advice, pressure, fear . . . just selling. Guess what. My numbers went up. That's when it hit me—selling is already hard. All this crap management insists on didn't help me succeed. Not only that, but once it was gone, I improved. It doesn't take a genius to figure out why.

No matter what role you're in, ask yourself, *Am I helping?* That's all that matters. I doubt I'll ever work another operating role, but if I do, I promise you I will entertain only one question about sales performance. *How can I help?* That doesn't mean we have no responsibility to explain our performance strategies, why we did what we did. That's fair. But I swear to you that not one time out of a million that people inserted themselves into my sales execution did they help. It only made it harder. So please, especially if you're not in sales, embrace this advice. Because it's true. Ask us, "How can I help?" Remember, sales is already hard enough, so don't make it harder.

Closed Cockpit

This is an expression I've only recently started using, and I wish I'd implemented the idea behind it sooner. I'll give you the same advice I'd give myself if I ever take another operating role: close the cockpit. This means the sales team's daily performance is not open to anyone for audit except sales leadership. This doesn't mean you won't let the rest of the company fly on the airplane; it simply means they're not welcome in the cockpit.

Here's why. It doesn't help. I've run engineering teams, finance teams, legal teams, product teams, and marketing teams. Does anyone ever sit down with the head of engineering and say, "It looks like you guys had some problems with your development. The code wasn't perfect the first time. You should do something about it."? Does anyone ever tell the company lawyers, "The lawyers from our customers redlined our contract. You should have written a better contract in the first place."? Of course not. These departments have complete control of their destiny. They decide what to work on and who gets hired or fired. They control 100 percent of their world. Sales, on the other hand, deals with this little thing called *the marketplace*. Read Ben Horowitz's book *The Hard Thing about Hard Things*. The marketplace is where all variability exists. I've lost deals because the customer died, their building caught on fire, their company was acquired, and a trillion other variables unfolded without my knowledge or control.

If you're in sales, happily answer questions about strategy, productivity, yield, and any other aspect of Shot Calling. It's all fair game as you're building out and executing your shots. But once the plane is off the ground, and you're flying your sales team forward, close the cockpit. It's unfair and completely counterproductive to have discussions about individual and team performance that include judgements about those individuals and teams. That's where I close the cockpit, and so should you. This was a trap of my own making, and I will not fall into it again.

THE THREE-POINT SHOT

In July 2011, I attended the quarterly Trend Micro executive meeting. Nineteen of us sat at a big table in a big conference room for three days to discuss what was working, what wasn't working, why it wasn't working, and how to fix it. Late on day two, the whole thing suddenly seemed pointless. I don't recall the exact impulse that led me to feel this way. It wasn't that anything was even wrong, but the meeting had become a grind. The same conversations about the same issues with the same drama, over and over. I couldn't shake this feeling, so I leaned over to my colleague, John Maddison, then Trend Micro's Cloud Security general manager.

"Is this really what we were meant to do with our lives?" I asked quietly.

John stared ahead for a few seconds, then looked at me.

"No."

That was the moment I knew something had to change. It wasn't the work; it was me. I was stuck with a mental model of the world that was sapping my drive to keep my seat at the table. It was only a matter of time before I would make excuses for feeling this way, like that I was burned out or just tired. I also knew it wouldn't be long until someone else would come along without my baggage and sing a different tune, so I decided to do something.

For years I have admired an executive named Dave DeWalt. I didn't know him in 2011, but he entered the cybersecurity industry when he was named McAfee CEO in April 2007. He scorched the earth with a strategy of rapid expansion and aggressive mergers and acquisitions, and it worked. In February 2011, Dave cemented his place as the leading CEO in all of cybersecurity when Intel acquired McAfee for $7.7 billion. Word on the street was that Dave had over fifty CEO offers after the acquisition.

A few days after the Trend Micro meeting, I was reading up on the details of the McAfee deal when it dawned on me—I could be the next Dave DeWalt. OK, not quite. But why couldn't I raise my game and get on a path like his?

I concluded that some kind of leadership limitation held me back, but I couldn't put my finger on it. After all, what was the difference between me and Dave DeWalt? I competed head-to-head with DeWalt's sales team, and my teams beat his. I'd had a lot of success, spearheading the acquisition of a small company called Third Brigade. As much as I thought I could perform like DeWalt, it was painfully obvious the industry didn't see me that way—I wasn't getting job offers like Dave was.

That's when I made the best decision of my business career, to bridge my gap and learn how to be a big-time leader like Dave. I researched leadership development programs and with the support of Trend Micro CEO Eva Chen applied to and was accepted into a Harvard Business School program called Authentic Leadership. A great deal of what you will learn in the Three-Point Shot chapter stems from my coursework. And I'll let you in on a little secret—one of the most important lessons I learned was just how stupid it is to try to lead like someone else.

P.S. I'm now an advisor with Dave DeWalt's cybersecurity consulting practice, Momentum Cyber.

The Burst

In August 2011, I attended VMWare's "VMWorld" conference in Las Vegas. I was US president of Trend Micro at the time, and we had a series of activities planned, including a welcome party for customers and partners. The hotel party was typical Vegas stuff—drinking, flood, gambling. Everything went according to plan until something unusual happened that changed how I thought about leadership from that point forward.

First, a little backstory. In 2004, I was Trend Micro's Eastern Region sales director. A kickass group of salespeople worked for me, one of whom was David Twilley, based in Atlanta, Georgia. David reported to me for about a year and did a great job driving performance in his territory. When I was promoted to sales vice president in 2005, David no longer reported directly to me. David continued to do a great job while I was running the US team until 2007, when I was promoted to the Global GM role you read about earlier. I wasn't as close to the US sales team during this assignment, but that changed when I asked to run US sales again in 2010. Upon returning to the US team, I learned that one of our sales reps endured the most challenging life experiences you could possibly imagine. That rep was David Twilley.

It's hard to process what happened to David, let alone imagine how he must have felt, but here's the story. It started in early 2010 when David and the Southeast Region sales team held a customer appreciation event. They chose whitewater rafting as their activity. The day of the event, the sales team and customers met at the designated launch site. Everyone began boarding the rafts, including David, but something wasn't right. All of a sudden, his chest felt tight. With apologies, he made his exit and drove straight to the emergency room. Within two hours, he underwent triple bypass surgery to save his life. Afterward, David told his doctor about almost boarding the raft.

"There are no emergency surgery centers in the middle of a river, David," his doctor said. "If you had left the dock, you would've died."

Holy shit.

But it gets worse.

When this happened, David was married with three young girls. He returned from his recovery, ramped his territory back up to speed, and got his life back on track. Tragedy struck again. His wife was diagnosed with late-stage breast cancer. Now he was the primary caregiver, managing his career, home, wife, and daughters. His instinct and love for his family kicked in, and as much as possible, they tried to live a normal life. They focused on the little things, taking life one day at time, enjoying whatever little pleasures were possible, like going out to dinner. They did that one night in fall 2010 and returned to a disturbance in their neighborhood. Police and fire personnel were everywhere. As they approached their house, the brutal reality of what had happened became painfully apparent. Their home with all their possessions had burned to the ground. Nothing was left. Not even a picture frame had survived. The memories of a lifetime, destroyed.

Holy shit.

And it gets worse.

Two months later on Christmas Eve, David's wife passed away.

I don't have the words to describe what that must have been like. David told this story at Trend Micro's January 2012 Sales Kickoff meeting. I asked him to because of the journey he'd been through. I consider it the proudest moment of my career. Six hundred people strained to hear every word as I asked David to describe how he emerged from this experience. How he got his life back. How he got back on top professionally. And how they, too, could become better salespeople—and people. You could've heard a pin drop.

This brings us full circle to the VMWare event in August 2011, eight months after David's wife passed and three months before the kickoff meeting. The unusual moment I shared with David in Las Vegas, I ended up calling "the Burst."

When I arrived at the customer event in Vegas around 8:00 p.m., the party was in full swing. It was the usual combination of customers, partners, and employees. My role was largely to pay for the drinks. I saw David busy with customers as soon as I arrived. I gave him a quick high five due to the exceptional performance he somehow delivered that year. David had endured the grieving process, and Trend Micro gave him the space he needed. Our CEO and founders were always supportive that way. By the start of Q2, David hit his stride and was on track to sell over $1 million for the quarter. This was a big milestone for any rep at Trend, which came with a $10,000 bonus and tons of bragging rights.

Everyone pulled for David to exceed that mark, and I called him a few times during the quarter to push him along. Anyone who's been in sales knows "it ain't over till it's over," but with a lot of effort and a little luck, he made it. One million in sales, ten grand bonus. David was back.

I spent about an hour working the room and had another gig to attend, so I began making my exit. I didn't get a chance to hang out with David, so I made a point to grab him before I left to shake his hand and congratulate him. He was near the door as I approached and extended my handshake, but he didn't extend his hand. Instead, he looked me in the eye, raised both arms over his head, and yelled "YEAHHHH-HHHHHH!!!" Remember the scene in *Braveheart* when Mel Gibson screamed "FREEDOMMMMMMM!" right before they disemboweled him? It was like that, minus the disembowelment.

In a single burst of emotion, David seemed to celebrate his achievement at the same time he released all the pain of the past twelve months. The burst caught me off guard, so I nodded to imply I understood where this came from. The truth is, I didn't understand until two months later when I attended the Authentic Leadership class at Harvard. Now whenever that class comes up in conversation, I tell everyone the same thing.

"Beg, borrow, or steal for the chance to go. It will be the best experience of your career."

So far, a grand total of zero people have taken my advice to attend Authentic Leadership. The reason isn't totally clear, but I suspect four possible reasons.

- Most people don't want to learn the truth that they aren't very good leaders.
- They're wedded to a belief system about leadership they don't want to disrupt.
- They already have power and feel threatened by ideas about using it the right way.
- Other excuses like cost, time, blah, blah, blah . . .

Authentic Leadership is taught primarily by Bill George, who has immense personal gravity.

Bill George is a senior fellow at Harvard Business School, where he has taught leadership since 2004. He is the author of: *Discover Your True North* and *The Discover Your True North Fieldbook, Authentic Leadership, True North, Finding Your True North, 7 Lessons for Leading in Crisis* and *True North Groups*.

Mr. George is the former chairman and chief executive officer of Medtronic. He joined Medtronic in 1989 as president and chief operating officer, was chief executive officer from 1991-2001, and board chair from 1996-2002. Earlier in his career, he was a senior executive with Honeywell and Litton Industries and served in the U.S. Department of Defense.

Mr. George has served on the boards of Goldman Sachs, ExxonMobil, Novartis, Target Corporation, and the World Economic Forum USA. He recently concluded his term as a trustee of the Mayo Clinic, and has been board chair for Allina Health System, Abbott-Northwestern Hospital, United Way of the Greater Twin Cities, and Advamed.

In 2014, the Franklin Institute awarded him the Bower Award for Business Leadership. He was elected to the National Academy of Engineering in 2012, and was named one of the "Top 25 Business Leaders of the Past 25 Years" by PBS; "Executive of the Year-2001" by the Academy of Management; and "Director of the Year-2001-02" by the National Association of Corporate Directors. In 2018, Bill was presented with the *Larry Foster Award for Integrity in Public Communication* by the Arthur W. Page Center. Mr. George is a CNBC Contributor and makes frequent appearances on television and radio.

He received his BSIE with high honors from Georgia Tech, his MBA with high distinction from Harvard University, where he was a Baker Scholar, and honorary PhDs from Georgia Tech, Mayo Medical School, University of St. Thomas, Augsburg College and Bryant University. During 2002-03 he was professor at IMD International and Ecole Polytechnique in Lausanne, Switzerland, and executive-in-residence at Yale School of Management.5

Everyone who applies for the class is aware of Bill's credentials. Hell, they're a big reason for choosing it in the first place. Bill truly is a leadership rock star. That made it all the more surprising when Bill started our class by apologizing for the failed leaders of the last one hundred years. There I was in a Harvard Business School classroom surrounded by senior leaders from around the world ready to become the next Dave DeWalt, and Bill basically called bullshit on us all. Huh?

Someone raised their hand and asked, "The class is called 'Authentic Leadership.' Are you saying the failed leadership of the last hundred years is due to inauthentic leadership?"

"Yes," Bill said.

The point of the course is to understand the difference between authentic and inauthentic leadership, including why authentic leadership is superior and how to bring it into your world. Before we dive into the lessons Bill taught me, I want to make it abundantly clear that I take no credit for them. This is simply my interpretation and practical application of what I learned.

I have paid a high price trying my best to be an authentic leader. The world is mostly run by inauthentic leaders who are perfectly willing to screw with you. The only criticism I have of Authentic Leadership is that the course didn't account for the antigravity maneuvers that inauthentic leaders use on their own people. But I do, and it's time we all start holding abusive leaders accountable.

Back to the class. Authentic Leadership is taught in two sections. The first is a journey of self-discovery where you work in a small group to identify your "crucible" and understand how it changes you for the rest of your life (read *True North: Discover Your Authentic Leadership* by Bill George to understand the power of the crucible). The second half is harder. It focuses on your "leadership purpose" in ways that demand you identify how you intend to put the principles of authentic leadership into practice.

---

5   "About Bill George." NASA. Accessed September 15, 2020. https://billgeorge.org/about.

To this day, I'm amazed at how hard it was to answer the simple question that Bill asked in class. "What is the purpose of your leadership?" I freely admit I also struggled to answer the first time he asked. I believe I gave the same absurd response that half the class gave, "to lead by example." That's the worst, most inauthentic response possible. Authentic leaders know that the people they lead aren't driven by the example of someone else's life; they're driven by the example of their own lives.

Since completing the course, I've tested many leaders with Bill's question. "What is your leadership purpose?" I ask. Most of the time, the amusing response I get is "What do you mean?" Think about that. If I ask any leader in business, "What is the purpose of engineering, marketing, and legal?" they'd all have an answer. Ask those same people about the purpose of their leadership, and you get crickets. Or the occasional "to lead by example" horseshit. The brutal truth is the vast majority of leaders have no purpose to their leadership; they're just the ones in charge. They are trained to manage, not to lead.

Here's how I summarize authentic leadership—it's the acceptance of your responsibility to unlock the passion and potential of those you lead. That's exactly what Bill George teaches in the class. That's also why I asked for Bill's help to understand what happened with David Twilley. I had a strong suspicion that understanding his burst was key to understanding my leadership purpose.

I was right.

Midway through the one-week class, I asked Bill for a few minutes of his time. I'm certain he has no memory of this conversation, but it was a defining moment in my leadership journey, and I remain grateful for his wisdom. After class on Wednesday, I told Bill about David and the events that culminated in the burst. I could never compare the tragedies David endured to the challenges we face in business, I explained. But it had been almost a year, and David and his daughters were prospering. I also told Bill I understood the burst as an emotional release, but how did it relate to leadership? It felt amazing to share that moment with David, but could it be replicated to unlock the potential of others?

What if my leadership purpose is to unlock the burst within every team?

Bill's response connected all the dots. Bear in mind this conversation took place in 2011, so I'm paraphrasing, but here's the essence.

"You were the one person who could give David what he needed," Bill told me. "After everything he went through, you represented the one person who could validate his triumph. What he released with that 'burst' was more of a feeling than an idea. That's why he just screamed it instead of trying to articulate it. Your position as his leader was the catalyst to unlock that feeling."

I told Bill I hadn't done much to "unlock" anything within David, I just encouraged him along the way. David did all the work. Bill looked at me the way a parent looks at a child when they finally realize what the parent was trying to teach them all along.

"Imagine what's possible if you actually lead."

That was my breakthrough moment. I decided my leadership purpose would be "to lead people to their burst." I wasn't sure exactly how I would execute on that purpose, but I've since figured it out.

One thing I did know that day was how stupid my prior leadership ideas were. Driving back from Cambridge, Massachusetts, I cried in the car thinking about the pain I'd caused. The ego and arrogance, the fear and control, the hubris and bullshit. Another thing I was entirely sure of was that trying to be Dave DeWalt was the dumbest idea of my life. Not because Dave isn't worth emulating. He is. But trying to copy someone else's leadership purpose is impossible. You must find your own leadership purpose because that's the only way it will ever be authentic to you. Fortunately, I found mine. Now it's your turn to find yours.

My Leadership Purpose

I died on October 30, 2011. Thankfully, I recovered.

A few weeks after I completed the Authentic Leadership class, Trend Micro held their annual leaders meeting called "Global Summit," beginning on October 29, 2011. One hundred and thirty-five people from around the world attended, all with the title "director" or higher, including our founder, Steve Chang. He'd heard about the leadership class I took at Harvard and wanted my thoughts.

At the beginning of the event, I sat down with Steve and described Authentic Leadership. I glowed as I told him how powerful the experience was. I shared my initial motive to "be like Dave" and how I realized the absurdity of that idea. I also told Steve the David Twilley "burst" story and how Bill George helped me realize its significance. Then I described how it all connected to reveal my leadership purpose. I was going to build an "Airforce," which is why most Trend executives found themselves in the seat of a fighter jet flying through the canyons of Los Angeles two days prior on October 28.

What the hell is a Trend Micro Airforce? Here's what. As I said earlier, on my drive back from Authentic Leadership, I realized I wasn't the leader I wanted to be. I swore to myself that I would become an authentic leader whose leadership purpose is to unlock the burst inside of us all. But it wasn't practical to start showing up to meetings asking people to "burst." I needed a legitimate business strategy behind my leadership purpose. It came together on the drive home.

In 2011, cloud computing was still a young industry, but we'd already decided that our objective at Trend Micro was to be "#1 in Cloud Security." Company leadership agreed to change our brand promise from "Securing Your Web World" to "Securing Your Journey to the Cloud." It wasn't hard to understand that the journey to the cloud was a massive, inevitable shift. We had to make changes if we were going to be successful in changing our legacy 1.0 sales culture to a modern 2.0 cloud culture. But how?

Here's how. I brought authentic leadership to our business strategy. I knew I had to get the entire sales team competent in cloud computing. I also wanted to unlock their potential and help them reach the moment where it burst forth as it had with David Twilley. It dawned on me that I could reframe our new brand promise. Reframing is a powerful concept from Authentic Leadership.

Instead of a salesforce that toiled on the ground, I could build an Airforce that sold in the clouds. I could motivate the entire group with a challenge—to join our Airforce and "earn your wings," you must complete a series of performance and development challenges. I would also inspire my direct reports to become authentic leaders in the process by giving them only one way to earn their wings—help each and every member of their teams earn theirs.

I had found my leadership purpose. I was going to build an Airforce. Not only did reframing our brand promise enable me to see my leadership purpose clearly, it made me feel differently about my leadership. I went from feeling stuck to feeling energized. The opportunity felt like a tremendous gift. Trend Micro was going to pay me to build an Airforce. How awesome is that!

Back to the conversation with Steve Chang. I explained the thought process that led to my leadership purpose. Just days before Global Summit, I convinced our executive team to help me promote the Earn Your Wings program by filming a video of the executives flying in the clouds. My marketing VP, Dan Woodward, found an outfit that specialized in making inspirational videos with a fighter jet theme. The idea was to use the video of Trend Micro executives flying around in fighter jets at the 2012 Sales Kickoff, the same one David Twilley would speak at, to build excitement for Earn Your Wings.

Steve now had the complete context of my Harvard experience, my leadership purpose, and the reason I had most of the executive team, including our CEO and his sister-in-law, flying a fighter jet in the skies above Los Angeles. The story captivated Steve. He wanted me to share it with everyone at the conference, so we rearranged the agenda.

On October 30, 2011, I addressed all 135 attendees. As usual, I relied on a caffeine hit from Diet Coke to get my energy up, and I told my story. I covered the David Twilley burst, my learnings from Authentic Leadership, and the reframing that led to my leadership purpose to build an Airforce. As I'm sure you know, most corporate events aren't riveting from a content perspective. This was different. For the first time in my life, I felt like I had something meaningful to add as a presenter. Not the typical rah rah rah, blah blah blah bullshit, but something that could make a difference. I could feel the audience internalizing my message.

I sensed an overwhelming desire to understand their leadership purpose and how they might reframe to find it.

After I finished, people lined up to talk to me. We would be at the conference for the next three days, so finding me to talk wouldn't be an issue. It didn't matter. I spent the next fifteen minutes talking to as many people as possible and returned to my seat so we could start the next session.

Then I died.

There is no real business virtue in what you're about to read. It's just so weird that I have to tell you what happened. After I sat down, I finished my Diet Coke. That's when I felt "the thing" occur. "The thing" is what my family calls vasovagal syncope, a disorder I had been diagnosed with almost twenty years earlier. Basically, it's a condition that can cause fainting based on triggers that are not always predictable. I'd been dealing with it most of my adult life by laying down when I felt the condition had been triggered. Most of my friends and co-workers had witnessed it at some point, so it wasn't that scary when I felt it come on at the conference. I simply turned to my friend Sanjay next to me and said, "Hey, dude. In about twenty seconds, it's pretty likely I'm going to pass out. Don't worry. It's just this condition I have. I'll be fine." Then the lights went out.

When I regained consciousness, the room was empty except for my CEO, Eva Chen, who was holding my hand, two paramedics, and another colleague named Dave Asprey. As they stood over me, I explained there was nothing to worry about. I had "the thing" and would be fine after a few minutes of rest. Dave insisted I tell what I'd had to eat or drink. I told him I'd had the normal food served at the conference. Oh, and the Diet Coke. That was the moment Dave Asprey probably saved my life.

Dave worked at Trend Micro, but outside of work, he was one of the world's most prolific biohackers. If Dave's name rings a bell, it's because he created a program called "The Bulletproof Executive" and is now CEO of Bulletproof 360, the makers of Bulletproof Coffee. Dave explained to me how Diet Coke can mess with you. The body can't tell the difference between real sugar and sugar substitutes, and under certain circumstances, substitute sugar can trigger an allergic reaction. Apparently, I had been unconscious for over ten minutes. David strongly suggested I see an allergist.

I recovered well enough to convince the paramedics I didn't need to go to the hospital. I participated in our team-building event that night, paintball. No way I was going to miss the chance to shoot my colleagues. Between the fighter jets, the storytelling, the passing out, Dave Asprey's insights, the fortune cookie, and the paintball, Global Summit 2011 was the weirdest event of my life.

I did see an allergist, and Dave was right. I'm allergic to substitute sugar. In certain circumstances, it triggers a reaction. I was not suffering from "vasovagal syncope" for the last twenty years, I was going into anaphylactic shock each time. After I told my allergist how I passed out and was unconscious for over ten minutes, she told me, "Technically, you died. And without immediate attention, less than half the people who are unconscious for that long come back to life." Holy. Shit.

My team worked on the Earn Your Wings program for the remainder of 2011, and we launched at our 2012 Sales Kickoff meeting in January. The event opened with the video of executives flying in fighter jets, then I took the stage and explained our theme. I said we needed to transform our skill set and embrace our new brand promise to help customers secure their journey to the cloud. I then introduced the Airforce and explained how each and every member of the team would be challenged to earn their wings. I told the David Twilley Las Vegas burst story. The burst was inside each of them, and the leadership team was committed to helping them unlock their full potential. Then I asked David to join me on stage.

The format for David's session was a simple interview. We both sat on stools, and I asked David to describe what was going through his head during the burst. Most people knew David had gone through tough times, but hardly anyone knew the full extent. I asked David to describe his journey, the one you read earlier. As David spoke, I felt the same sensation I'd had at Global Summit—*I'm doing something really important*.

I later learned the audience rated my presentation the highest of any executive who spoke that day. Trend Micro had a very talented group of executives, four of whom are elite presenters. For the first time in my career, I'd outscored everyone. I didn't suddenly become great at presenting, I just had a story that stirred people's emotions. That's the only public speaking advice I can give, by the way.

As I said earlier, the interview with David was the proudest moment of my career. I concluded the session by describing how everyone could earn their wings. I announced that, upon earning your wings, you'd receive a $5,000 bonus. Applause and cheers gave away people's excitement. As we finished, I announced a surprise for David. To honor his personal journey and his contribution to our new theme, I officially inducted David Twilley as the first member of the Trend Micro Airforce. I handed David a check for $5,000. As I pinned David's wings on his jacket, six hundred people gave him a long, rousing standing ovation. In those few moments on stage with David, I realized I'd never seen a human being look so validated.

Your Leadership Purpose

The Earn Your Wings program was my first official leadership strategy with a defined purpose. When I resigned from Trend Micro six months later to pursue a new opportunity, I didn't have confidence in the incoming leader replacing me to carry the program forward. All my leadership strategies are underpinned with authentic leadership principles, so I knew the new leader's fear-and-control approach would undermine my strategy. I simply decided it was better to end Earn Your Wings rather than have it undermined by a Kabuki Dancer, so that's what I did.

I've implemented authentic leadership strategies at every company I've been at since Trend Micro. Like all strategies, there is risk. Your goal with any leadership purpose should be to maximize the chance of success. Trust me, it's not easy to overcome the antigravity of inauthentic leaders. If I did anything wrong with my leadership strategies, it's that I failed my own Three *R*s Test and did not convince other leaders to adopt authentic leadership. I wish I could go back in time with the Shot-Caller framework, but fortunately, you can avoid my mistakes and get leadership right the first time. Here's how.

The Sweet Spot

The reason authentic leadership is superior is the concept of "the sweet spot." This will also explain why this chapter is called the Three-Point Shot. By now, you should have etched in your memory that there are three forms of value. The sweet spot breaks down human performance into three categories as well. Note the overlap between the three forms of value and the three elements of the sweet spot. Think of this combination as the Shot Caller's version of the sweet spot.

- **Capability**: This is equivalent to functional value. This element poses the question "Does the individual possess the capability to perform at a high level?"
- **Passion**: This is equivalent to emotional value. It poses the question "Is the individual emotionally invested in his or her role?" I prefer "emotional investment" over "passion" because passion isn't required to reach your sweet spot. Emotional investment is.
- **Value**: This is equivalent to economic value, so I prefer to call this element "worth." It poses the questions "Is the individual adding sufficient economic value? Does the individual perceive his or her contribution as equitably compensated?" Basically, employer and employee ask themselves "Is it worth it?"

The sweet spot is how Bill George describes all three elements—capability, passion, value—intersected at a high level. When people are good at their jobs, both parties perceive the economic exchange of value as worth it, and they are emotionally committed to their roles. Here's an illustration of the sweet spot, which I also refer to as the performance zone.

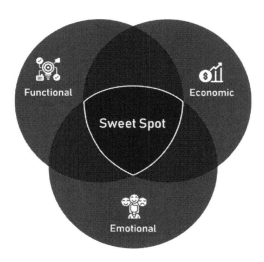

Figure 4.1 The Performance Zone.

The sweet spot is not a leadership theory. The data is clear—individuals operating in the sweet spot outperform anyone who is not. The problem is that only 8 percent of individuals self-identify as being in their sweet spot! This is the tragedy of failed leadership. Ninety-two percent of us do not have our potential unlocked by our leaders. With few exceptions, I have not experienced leadership that understands *how* to get people into their sweet spot, let alone have the desire to do so. Let's change that. Please . . . I am begging you . . . if you take *one* action after reading this book, let it be a commitment to an authentic leadership purpose that helps people reach their sweet spot. Nothing in business is more rewarding, I promise you.

Authentic Leadership Principles

Defining your leadership purpose is mostly about sticking to the guiding principles of leadership. Of course, these are my guiding principles, and while I've endured some suffering trying to honor them, they have never let me down.

Leadership Principle 1: No Jerks Allowed

Seriously, this is a defining requirement of good leaders. "Don't be a jerk," doesn't mean you cannot demand results, it simply means your actions must have a constructive, authentic purpose behind them. If you can't commit to that, you will never be an authentic leader—or a Shot Caller. If you feel the need to be a jerk, put down this book, go outside, and play hide-and-go-screw yourself. No jerks allowed.

Leadership Principle 2: Unlock the Passion and Potential of Those You Lead

I believe I can help anyone from any country in any role thrive as long as I adhere to this second principle. I accomplish this by helping people find their sweet spot where they're in the best position to realize their maximum potential. It requires no special training or effort to make this happen. You just have to eliminate fear and use positive reinforcement. After all, how hard is it to do these three things?

- **Function**: Train and enable people to be highly skilled at their work.
- **Emotional Investment**: Reinforce the relationship between a person's role and the company's or department's mission. Then motivate the mission by making people feel how much their contribution to success is inspirational and appreciated.
- **Worth**: Pay people what they're worth to you. If compensation is out of whack, fix it.

That's all it takes to get people headed toward their sweet spot.

Leadership Principle 3: Be Authentic

It's embarrassing this needs to be a basic leadership principle. I'm reminded of the question Bill George fielded on day one—"Are you saying the failed leadership of the last one hundred years is due to inauthentic leadership?" He answered yes. So would I now, if asked. Authentic leaders accept their responsibility to unlock the passion and potential of those they lead. But what does it mean to be authentic? I'm not going to give you the Harvard definition of authentic leadership, just mine. I define authenticity as "constructive connections."

Any time you exercise your leadership, you connect your message to the business principle at stake with Shot Calling. What the hell does that mean? If I'm talking to a sales manager about performance, I frame it as a discussion about our product-level forecast, which is essential to the Kill Shot. That connects our conversation to the business purpose that everyone is well versed in and brings consistency to your leadership.

Next, be constructive any time you give feedback. There is no place in business for destructive feedback. Anyone who leads that way should be subject to "hostile workplace" legal action. Constructive feedback always includes positive reinforcement for work done well before examining any deficiencies. Follow these guidelines to deliver constructive feedback:

- Recognize the person's worth to the business.
- Explain your deep desire to help and apologize for the company's failure to have presented the need for the conversation in the first place.
- Explain exactly where the deficit is using as much data as available, connecting to both the individual and the big picture.
- Give the person the chance to explain why the deficit exists.
- Discuss expectations to get back on track and get their buy-in.
- Tell them you believe in them and won't bullshit them. You expect them to reach their full potential, and you will help every step of the way.
- Make sure they realize they're a part of the bigger picture and that everyone is depending on and rooting for them. But they must do their part.

- Celebrate little wins along the way and validate their progress. The same way I was David Twilley's source of validation, so, too, are you for the people you lead.

Does your manager offer feedback along these guidelines? Unfortunately, there is a 92 percent chance your answer is no. It's hard to explain why there is so much bad leadership. When I practiced the authentic leadership I preach at one cybersecurity company, the CEO told me, "Your problem is you're too nice." What the hell? I couldn't change his mind. Kabuki Dancers like him are the reason I'm writing this book, to create Shot Callers who accept that their leadership purpose is to honor the three principles of authentic leadership. Now it's up to you. Are you with me, or are you with the Kabuki Dancers?

Your Leadership In Action

Now that you've embraced your leadership purpose, put it into action. That's what I did with Earn Your Wings. Don't be surprised to see your general leadership purpose evolve once you do this. In my case, my general purpose—to unlock the passion and potential of those I lead—evolved into the specific strategy to transform my sales team through the Airforce program.

Every time I've started a new chapter in my leadership journey, I've anchored my strategy in the three foundational principles and aligned them with the shots being called. You must use some discretion here. Unless you are CEO, you won't be able to simply execute your strategy. You must build consensus and at times reframe your leadership strategy to something within your control. I usually frame my leadership strategies to match my job scope—an overall strategy for the entire department with separate strategies as needed for teams who need more.

The key to putting your leadership into action is the Shot-Caller sweet spot. Remember, your leadership should improve functional, emotional, and economic effectiveness. Here are examples of leadership strategies I've used to affect all three.

Functional Leadership Strategy: Earn Your Wings

You read about this in detail, so let's not rehash particulars. The skill set upgrade required to get Trend Micro's entire US sales team capable of selling cloud security solutions was entirely functional. Anytime you need to improve the functional capability of a team or individual, use training and enablement. These could include incentives for achieving the desired outcome like we did with Earn Your Wings. An essential part of any functional capability improvement strategy is a grading system. You need to establish a certification process and demand that people achieve it.

The biggest trap when executing strategies to affect individual capability is the perception they shouldn't need the strategy in the first place. The entrapper is usually someone who already has high functional skill. They push the naive narrative that instead of "training and trusting," it's better to "step in and lead" to the desired outcome.

This problem appears in *Good to Great* by Jim Collins, who describes five levels of leadership. Level two, three, and four leaders often can't resist their shortcomings and insist on "grabbing the ball" because they have a warped understanding of their leadership purpose. Instead of unlocking potential, they define their leadership purpose in terms of putting themselves at the center of the desired outcome. Instead of individuals learning how to be more capable, they only learn how to get out of the boss's way.

I'm not saying an authentic leader never steps in. They should when necessary based on constructive analysis. However, you will create systemic weakness if you don't build teams capable of getting the job done, so don't fall into that trap.

Emotional Investment Leadership Strategy: Guardians of the Galaxy

This leadership strategy wasn't planned. It just happened through a series of events. When I arrived at Emailage, they did not have a sales ops team, so I had to build one from scratch. The best candidate to lead the team was a young guy named Anthony Enrico, who was running the customer success team. Anthony has an MBA and the skill set to get the job done right. It took a little convincing, but Anthony agreed to take the role.

I don't recall when this conversation unfolded, but in an early meeting with Anthony and the team he put together, they updated me on their progress. I could tell they were competent, and there was no compensation inequity. But I sensed they were not emotionally invested in their roles. I have significant experience building and running sales ops teams, and I know just how vital their function is to any high-performing sales organization. No way I was going to start my role without Anthony's team realizing how important theirs were.

That's when I told Anthony's team, "Look, you all have to understand something. If you fail, we're screwed. Orders won't process, deals won't get done, commissions won't get paid, forecasts will fail, and the world will end. From this point forward, you are no longer sales ops, you are the Guardians of the Galaxy!"

The impact was instant. Framed as sales ops, the team felt like low-level plumbers there to make water flow through pipes. Framed as Guardians of the Galaxy, the team felt like superheroes who protected Emailage from great perils. They embraced their new identity with high energy. The superheroes became their brand. When we were acquired by LexisNexis, I told them our sales ops team was so strong we referred to them as Guardians of the Galaxy. LexisNexis loved it.

Anthony and his team went from emotional underinvestment in sales ops to passion for being the Guardians. This strategy wasn't planned, didn't take more than a moment to execute, and didn't cost the company a dime. Yet when I asked the Guardians what their identity meant to them, Anthony said, "That was the single-best decision you made at Emailage."

The trap to avoid when executing on emotional investment strategies is being uninspiring. "The Guardians" worked because the team could relate to it. Everybody likes superheroes. The brand was cool and connected the team to the mission. Anytime you ask for more emotional investment, make sure that people can internalize your strategy, feel positive about it, and grasp the business connection. Without these three, your strategy will not have the desired effect. Here are the Guardians.

Economic Leadership Strategy: Director-Driven Incentives

Remember, economic leadership is about worth. Is it worth it to both parties to exchange value? The question you face as a leader is whether or not there is a sense of equity between the employer and the employee. Tension occurs whenever there is imbalance, so you must account for this reality with a strategy that preserves the feeling of equity that keeps people in their sweet spot.

At Trend Micro, my economic leadership strategy was Director-Driven Incentives (DDIs). Sales managers designed quarterly incentives for sales reps. I was explicit about packaging these extra incentives as "director driven," meaning the reps knew their managers controlled the incentives. This strategy allows for the inevitable drift that occurs with incentive plans, which often causes feelings of inequity and tension. DDIs allowed the managers to adjust for this drift each quarter using targeted incentives. It worked.

Since "worth" is what someone perceives is a fair value exchange, the economic leadership strategy trap is that you simply can't afford the strategy in the first place. I'm a fan of compensating for perceived inequity in ways that don't cost much or sometimes any money. Just be careful. The person who perceives inequity must be made to feel that the compensating treatment creates equity. They must feel that the "employee of the month" or other noncompensated recognition creates equity. That it allows them to feel like the exchange of value is worth it because recognition of their contribution brings balance. If it doesn't, you'll end up no better off than where you started, so please do not fall into this trap.

Tension Management

Earlier, you read about the time I spent at MIT with Steve Chang studying tension management. Most of this section comes from that class, so it's bulletproof. I've used this tension management approach in many business situations and consider it the best way to deal with change or conflict and the inevitable tension they create.

Once you start calling your shots, there will be tension. The more effective your tension management skills, the better the outcome. More importantly, tension is almost always predictable. As you call your shots, ask yourself, *Will this cause tension?* and have a plan to deal with it. That's why I don't buy this "failure to execute" bullshit. You can see tension coming from a mile away. Any failure to respond is almost always traceable to flaws in one or more of your shots, not in their execution.

I've taught the Shot Caller's approach to tension management to teams many times. What you're about to read is condensed and by no means comprehensive. Feel free to explore this topic beyond this book, but for the last ten years, I've relied on just this advice because it's simple and it works. In short, tension shows up in three forms: healthy, unhealthy, and oscillating. Your job is to identify the tension type you're dealing with and respond accordingly. Here's how.

Healthy Tension

Exactly as labeled, healthy tension occurs anytime a human system must absorb beneficial change. Positive change does not mean there won't be any tension, it just means that leadership needs to carry the torch long enough for the change to permeate. A common healthy tension management strategy is training. No one wants to take time to get trained, but in the long run, everyone accepts that it's necessary and beneficial.

Whether training or not, use these three keys to get people to absorb healthy tension:

- **Focus on outcome.** Humans, whether we like or not, run their own version of the Three *R*s Test when asked to invest time and energy in anything. They need to believe the endeavor is worth it, or it will fail, no matter how much you try to shove an initiative down their throats. Provide as much data as you can so they can rationalize that the outcome is worth it.
- **What's good for the goose is good for the gander.** This expression means if you're going to ask people to absorb tension, you'd better be willing to absorb it yourself. Please don't make the mistake of calling this "leading by example." This isn't leadership. It's a way to make people feel something is worth it be-

cause their boss is doing it too. Call it whatever you want. "Eat your own dog food." "Practice what you preach." "Good for the goose." Just don't call it leadership. It's tension management, and good leaders know how to do it.

- **Reaffirm the initiative's value.** Years ago, I had an EVP of sales at Infonet named John Hoffman. Great guy and tremendous leader. John was known for saying, "If it ain't worth measuring, it ain't worth doing." This is true anytime you ask people to absorb tension. At Emailage, we asked everyone to go through an intense sales enablement program. Afterward, we saw our conversion rates improve by 90 percent for unweighted pipelines and 60 percent for weighted pipelines. We reaffirmed the value of our investment from the board on down. All the tension of that program was fully absorbed and totally healthy.

Unhealthy Tension

This is the easiest tension to manage because there's no need to figure out what to do. Eliminate it. The trick is to spot unhealthy tension early enough so it doesn't become toxic and result in the third form of tension, oscillating tension. Here are three keys for managing unhealthy tension.

- **Use the Three *R*s Test.** We all know the experience of going down some rat hole because the boss wanted us to. I could describe a hundred different times I was tasked to pursue some stupid initiative because of a promised amazing outcome. There was never any real chance to succeed, no data to support the effort, and no best practice deeming it necessary. Just some Kabuki Dancer who thought it was a good idea. If your initiative can't pass the Three *R*s Test, it's not going to be healthy. Worse yet, if you force it on people, you'll create the dreaded oscillating tension problem you'll read about next.
- **Fail fast.** I don't have a single memory of grinding out a bad idea that turned out great. I have dozens of memories of grinding

on something I thought was a bad idea that I wish I would've quit sooner. Knowing if something is going to succeed or fail is what Shot Calling is all about. Don't waste your time unless you're taking shots you know you have a good chance to make.

- **Have courage.** Sometimes it's hard to tell the bosses they're wrong. I've done it many times, sometimes resulting in my own demise. I used to care about being generous in the face of a demonstrably bad idea. Now I just don't give a shit. No matter what role you're contributing from, everyone benefits when a tension-causing bad idea is eliminated.

Oscillating Tension

Oscillating tension occurs anytime you ask a human system to absorb something that isn't worth it in the first place yet isn't so bad that the humans flat-out reject it. Instead, tension lingers, an irritant that won't go away. Ultimately, it becomes "noise." Here are three keys to dealing with oscillating tension.

- **Remember this formula: P = P − I (Performance = Potential minus Interference).** Steve Chang, founder of Trend Micro, taught his team this equation many years ago. I teach it to my teams now, and so should you. It might seem odd that you have to teach people that noise is bad, but you must. This equation says it all. It's aligned with authentic leadership. Say it like this, "If we become Shot Callers, if we embrace authentic leadership, and if we don't become 'mass-holes' by being the source of noise, we can unlock our full potential and realize maximum performance." A mass-hole is anyone who reduces gravity within their own company. Pro tip: Don't be a mass-hole.
- **No jailbreaks!** A jailbreak is what happens when humans react to noise ineffectively. Instead of working as a team to courageously identify and fix tension, they go around it. "Don't like

the process? Go around it." "Don't like my boss? Go around them." "Don't agree with the strategy? Go around it."

Startups are especially vulnerable to this problem because building something out of nothing is largely one giant jailbreak, at least in the beginning. Then it gets toxic. Jailbreaks don't scale. They undermine Shot Calling. They break trust in leadership, and sooner or later, the business breaks.

The trick to managing through this is to include everyone in Shot Calling from the beginning. Teach people why jailbreaks are so harmful and help them get better. Never reward jailbreaking unless someone did the right thing and helped identify and fix the cause of tension. However, if someone is simply calling their own shots instead of yours, you must get rid of the person or risk the chronic underperformance that comes from the oscillating tension they create.

- **Indulgence kills companies.** The "servant leadership" philosophy is the polar opposite of indulgence. Leadership largely consists of manically driven people with huge egos who end up with all the power. What could possibly go wrong? For better or worse, every thought, idea, strategy, whim, impulse, or urge gets indulged because they have power and are willing to use it.

Ask anyone who knows me how willing I am to call bullshit on indulgent behavior. I've been fired for doing it, but I couldn't help myself. Indulgence kills companies. Indulgers are nothing more than Kabuki Dancers with power. They're the sworn enemies of Shot Callers. You don't need to indulge whims and urges. You're a Shot Caller; you're too busy taking (and making) your shots.

Current State, Desired State

You've read about reframing, the powerful technique of looking at something differently to reveal its true value. I offer you the "current state, desired state" construct as the best way to have any business conversation about issues, problems, or concerns you need to address. I spent many years trying to have these conversations in an unstructured way. Too often, the conversation got derailed. There was typically too much emotion and not enough constructive dialogue about how to solve the problem. Since I first encountered this easy-to-use framework to have discussions, I have never *not* used it. Current state, desired state reframed my view on dialoguing with people so that uncomfortable, difficult issues can become empowering and productive.

One ground rule before you learn this framework. This is for discussions that relate to <u>execution after you've called your shots</u>. Current state, desired state implies that every company from the smallest to the largest has only five levers to drive performance from the current state to the desired state. The five levers are structure, process, people, tools, and incentives.

In fact, I insist my team commit them to memory and hear them in their sleep. *Structure, process, people, tools, incentives, structure, process, people, tools, incentives, structure, process, people, tools, incentives . . .* You get the idea.

The levers are simple to pull. With any issue related to execution, you simply ask, "What's the current state?" Then ask, "What's our desired state?" Then you pull all five levers. The trick, of course, is how. Current state, desired state is a massive subject, so I'm going to give you my go-to principles that guide me on all five. These first principles of altering performance have never let me down.

Structure

Guiding Principle: The shortest distance between two points is a straight line.

I've been a part of every conceivable structure in business—direct, indirect, overlay, matrix, joint. You name it, and I've worked in it, designed it, or run it. Whenever possible, create direct lines of reporting and avoid every other structure. Exceptions only make sense when they drive efficiency because they rarely enhance performance.

Think about your Moonshot, Kill Shot, and Money Shot. Then add what you've learned about the Three-Point Shot. All shots go together. Indirect lines of reporting show nothing more than a lack of understanding of the shots being called. Once you realize you don't have to guess what to execute, nothing offers crisper execution with less tension than direct lines of reporting.

While we're on the subject, corporate structures are a joke. Dividing people into teams based on function is a five-thousand-year-old war strategy. I would change all of it if within my power. In my world, no company would have teams except Moonshot, Kill Shot, Money Shot, Three-Point Shot, and the Whole Shot. I'd also eliminate the CEO role. It's limiting to give so much power to one person when most CEOs don't know how to use it. Most CEOs don't call their shots, they block those who do. Within my org structure, you could have a chief executive, but the "shot team" leaders would not report to them. Each shot team lead would have no boss; the leaders would work as a team of equals like the knights of Camelot's round table. The King Arthur role would be an oversight executive known as the Chief Gravity Officer whose sole responsibility is to evaluate how well the shot team leaders execute their respective shots and how well the teams act as a unifying force. The first company to implement Shot Calling within this structure would be unstoppable.

This comes up all the time in my world so I will offer one one more point of guidance for your Shot-Calling org structure. Which team should own product marketing? Simple. If your inner core is functional value, put product marketing with the product or engineering teams. If your inner core is emotional, put it in marketing.

Process

Guiding Principle: Brakes make the race car go faster, not slower.

I'm a trained race car driver, so I know firsthand this is true. Brakes are as important as the gas pedal and are in many ways more important. Sure, you can "put the pedal to the metal" to start, but at the first turn, you're going to crash and burn unless you brake. The best drivers use the break and the gas in tandem. That's how you win the race.

Process is just like that. You want enough to get the job done but not so much that it slows you down unnecessarily. Tapping the breaks as you're flying down the straightaway is not necessary. Breaking before you crash into the wall is.

People

Guiding Principle: *300.*

I love the movie *300*. The few stand against the many. But these three hundred soldiers were not the ordinary few. These were Spartans, warriors so dedicated to their mission that anything felt possible. Shot Callers are the Spartans of business. This book is about creating Shot Callers. Be a Shot Caller. Create Shot Callers. No other strategy for people I know of has a bigger impact.

Tools

Guiding Principle: It's not about what works, it's about what works for you.

I'm a tool junkie. I frequently take calls from vendors offering new apps, software, and systems that can help me win. My rule is that any professed gain must improve the current state by at least 25 percent, or it's not worth it.

With that in mind, I've also shut down many new tool initiatives. That's because many are overkill, don't perform well enough, or cause too much tension that the humans can't absorb. I've gone from spreadsheet-based commission administration to cloud-based and from the cloud back to spreadsheets simply because one worked better for us than the other.

Don't get hung up on the latest tools. I recently piloted an AI tool for lead scoring, and it couldn't outperform the most basic human effort on the same task. I've seen many "see a problem, buy a tool" reactions, and before you know it, you're distracted from the mission. Find the balance between what works, what can be absorbed, and what adds at least 25 percent uplift before investing in a new tool.

However, don't delude yourself. You can't compete if you are out-gunned because your competitor has the right tools and you don't. It blows me away that anyone thinks they can compete without Sales-force.com, for instance. You can't. So be smart—get tools that work and work for you.

Incentives

I have never had a 100 percent salary job in my life. I've operated under, written, or otherwise been a part of virtually every compensation strate-gy known to exist. I've also studied incentive strategy and worked with the world's most renowned consulting company on incentives many times. There is no perfect way to structure any incentive strategy. They all come with trade-offs, so I'll give you a few more guiding principles because this subject demands it. I live by these principles, and they've never steered me wrong.

Guiding Principles:

- **Rewards are not incentives.** Remember, rewards compensate for achieving specific outcomes that don't require behavior change. Incentives compensate for behavior changes. Don't mix them up. For example, if you're releasing a new solution and want your teams to become proficient at selling it, offer an in-centive to get better at selling the new solution. Don't simply offer a reward to the high achievers. It's never the high achievers who make you successful. Too many low achievers drag down overall performance. Understand what you're trying to affect be-cause most of the time you'll get what you pay for.

- **Keep it simple, keep it relevant.** I've been the victim of so many stupidly complicated incentive plans that I can't count them all. This is what happens when Kabuki Dancers decide incentives. Typically, there isn't anything wrong with the math; they all add up in the end. But by the time someone figures out how the incentive works, the relationship between the incentive and the outcome is lost, and you're just wasting money. The same happens when incentives are stretched out over too long a period. The feeling that it's worth it to try harder or alter behavior is essential to any incentive strategy. That feeling wears off if there isn't a reasonable time frame (e.g., one quarter) to receive the incentive.
- **Pay the Harmony Tax.** That's what I call an incentive strategy that balances "worth inequity." There are a million situations where you may want to pay the Harmony Tax, but the goal is always the same. Get people in their sweet spot. Sometimes it takes money to achieve that, but it's almost always money well spent.

Storming, Forming, Norming

Introduced in 1965, storming, forming, norming is a tried-and-true concept about team development. I'm sure you've heard it before, but I've put the Shot-Calling spin on it. The concept works well to help you understand and predict inevitable tension in business. Keep in mind, this is a surface-level use of this concept, so go deeper if you feel it's necessary. I haven't had to and still get a ton of value from it. Storming, forming, norming aligns with the three forms of value; that's my hypothesis, not settled science. Regardless, it still works.

Storming

This is the phase where the current state is so undefined that you're starting from scratch. It's when humans are trying to figure out what might work, so it's heavy on the development of function. It doesn't matter what you're working on—if it's new, you're going to storm through different ideas, often referred to as brainstorming. You may be wondering why the storming phase isn't more aligned to emotion than function. After all, don't emotions run high during a storm? Yes, but only once suggestions about form bubble up. That's a tell for spotting the transition between storming and forming.

Through all three phases, ask, "What's the current state?" and "What's the desired state?" Then use structure-process-people-tools-incentives to progress from one phase to the next. You should also identify the risk level of tension. What is your plan to ensure tension is successfully absorbed? Tension may have its root cause in any of the five areas, but it's always the people who feel it as opposed to a process or tool. Human nature predicts that people always serve their own interests through any group development exercise, so be on the lookout for self-serving agendas. I try to keep names out of boxes as these phases unfold, meaning we defer decisions about authority and reporting as long as possible. That way, it's difficult for anyone to ignore the needs of the group in favor of what they believe is best for them as an individual.

When I've added lead generation teams at several companies, we always had to deal with tension. Let's use that initiative as an example of how to storm successfully.

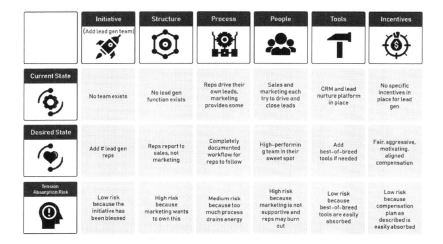

	Initiative (Add lead gen team)	Structure	Process	People	Tools	Incentives
Current State	No team exists	No lead gen function exists	Reps drive their own leads, marketing provides some	Sales and marketing each try to drive and close leads	CRM and lead nurture platform in place	No specific incentives in place for lead gen
Desired State	Add # lead gen reps	Reps report to sales, not marketing	Completely documented workflow for reps to follow	High-performing team in their sweet spot	Add best-of-breed tools if needed	Fair, aggressive, motivating, aligned compensation
Tension Absorption Risk	Low risk because the initiative has been blessed	High risk because marketing wants to own this	Medium risk because too much process drains energy	High risk because marketing is not supportive and reps may burn out	Low risk because best-of-breed tools are easily absorbed	Low risk because compensation plan as described is easily absorbed

Figure 4.2 Successful storming example: Lead generation.

I've kept this basic but realistic. You can see that most risk in this example comes from structure, process, and people.

- Structure tension: whether or not marketing can live with a structure where they don't own this function.
- Process tension: whether or not there is too much bureaucracy associated with getting the job done.
- People tension: whether or not lead generation reps can avoid burnout from a hard job.

Once you've identified where the tension risk is likely to come from, you can adjust. In this example, I'd spend extra time with marketing rationalizing why the lead gen team should live in sales. I'd also design an incentive strategy to reduce job burnout.

During the storming phase, be open minded and uncritical. The key to alleviating tension as you go through this and the other two phases is to apply the Three *R*s Test:

- Can you rationalize the functional value of the initiative?

- Can you resolve the human need to feel superior or at least satisfied?
- Does the majority conclude that the initiative is worth it?

Humans test anything of value this way, especially structural or authority-related decisions. It's literally the birthplace of tension, which carries forward if you can't pass the Three Rs Test.

Forming

Any initiative requiring human cooperation that emerges from the storming phase is "version 1.0." I use this analogy to imply that if there is a better version to be had, we make the changes needed to upgrade. In the forming phase, perceptions about winners or losers emerge because this phase formalizes authority and power. That's why forming is so <u>emotional</u>. Being flexible is critical because tensions mount in this phase.

In my experience, forming exercises make people get defensive if they believe they're going to end up with the short end of the stick. Reassure people that any version of structure or authority will evolve and account for everyone's emotional needs as best as possible. If your attempt to form what you stormed is met with noise, you have to go back, retake, and pass the Three Rs Test, like it or not.

Norming

Normal is the absence of noise—this is the *most* important outcome of tension management. Normal aligns with the worthiness of your initiative. You've succeeded in reaffirming the worthiness of the structure, so noise is no more. The key to reaching normal is you cannot skip your way here. You must storm and form or you will fail. Every time.

Use the guidance I've given you to storm, then form, then norm, taking and passing the Three Rs Test during each phase. Once you execute a few initiatives with this approach, you'll learn how easy it is to ease tension before it pulls your company apart. Just remember that there is no perfect version of normal. In my example, we structured lead generation to report to sales. In your case, it might make more sense to have them report to marketing. The right answer is the one you can normalize in your environment—and the one that gives you the best chance to reach the desired state.

Kabuki Culture

I've spent twenty-seven years at four companies and eight years among another eight companies. I've worked in organizations with over a hundred thousand people and those with fewer than fifty. I've experienced IPOs and total collapses. I've been an entry-level individual contributor and a C-level executive. Through it all, Human Resources people have attempted to convince me that culture exists, it matters, and that I'm somehow under its prescribed influence.

This cultural influence is usually described in some document, on some poster, or on the website. At Trend Micro, we professed to value the "3Cs, I, and T," which stand for customer, change, collaboration, innovation, and trust. Among other things, Google wants their culture "built on data" with "innovation prioritized." And of course there is the poster child and symbol of all culture investments: ping pong tables. So we do all these "culture-building" activities, and wealthy companies like Google get high marks on culture. Meanwhile, 92 percent of us aren't working in our sweet spot. Why the hell not?

The answer is we all live in Kabuki cultures. This book is about building a system for business and personal success. I've attempted to fill the void formed by the absence of anything like Shot Calling. This void keeps 92 percent of us outside our sweet spot. Why the hell should we be surprised? Most people work for leaders guilty of Kabuki dancing their way through some (or all) of these organizational flaws:

- Zero innovation process
- Obscure or irrelevant vision
- Absurd or ignored mission
- No understanding of core value or value stacking
- Incompetent application of strategy
- Weak or misguided brand promise
- Confusing value stack proposition
- Inability to pass the Three *R*s Test
- No understanding of the buyer's journey
- Warped beliefs about the sales profession
- Destructive ideas about maximizing human potential
- Inauthentic or incompetent leadership
- Abuse of or overindulgence in power

Sound familiar? It's a miracle that even 8 percent have found our sweet spots. To fill this massive void in a company, we're told to value abstracts like *communication*, *trust*, or *innovation*. As opposed to what? Do we need to be told that these are virtuous? As if without the guidance we'd value miscommunication, backstabbing, or stagnation?

When I studied Authentic Leadership at Harvard Business School, we learned the meaning behind the expression "me to we." It's shifting perspective from the individual to the team. Grasping the higher purpose of the collective is essential to success. Focus on the "we" instead of just "me" is a critical aspect of our leadership. I agreed then and agree now that it's the right idea. But what does the "we" even mean? What force binds individuals into a group? Incentives? Culture? Fear? Common purpose?

No number of posters, town hall meetings, company picnics, 360-degree reviews, or employee engagement surveys can fill the void formed by the lack of a system like Shot Calling. We don't need to go from "me to we." We need to go from "me to Shot Calling." Posters, picnics, and surveys are not necessarily bad as long you understand you are merely putting lipstick on a ping pong table.

Real culture emerges in the presence of a system everyone embraces—and that actually works. Imagine an entire company understanding how to take all five shots. The culture that would emerge would be incredibly communicative, trusting, innovative, and every other attribute you'd ever desire. You wouldn't need to convince people how it should feel to work there. They would *all* feel like Shot Callers. Because they would be.

But you cannot get there starting with "culture." That's insane. Investing in culture hasn't worked and never will. The *only* way to build an amazing culture is to fix the problems caused by Kabuki Dancers who don't have a system for success. Shot calling is the best possible investment you can make if you want an awesome culture.

I offer Shot Calling as such a system. I didn't create it for my health. I created it because there is nothing else out there, and I'm frustrated and exhausted by raging against Kabuki Dancers. Please help me fix this—become a Shot Caller. Or create a better system. I promise you, I'll be the first to use it!

Kabuki Dancer Tells

"The road to hell is paved with good intentions." That's the best defense I can mount on behalf of Kabuki Dancers. They mean well. That doesn't prevent them from dragging us into hell, but given a better way, they'll usually adjust. In the meantime, it pays to spot Kabuki dancing in action so you can stop it. Here are my tips for identifying Kabuki Dancer culture.

Gravity Stealing

This move is usually performed by people with a lot of authority. Powerful people are Kabuki Dancers if they can't stand letting go of that power. They have to be heard in every meeting. They do all the talking on a sales call. They make sure everyone knows how they feel. They indulge nearly every impulse. They often have a history of firing a lot of people. All the while, they accrue whatever gravity they can to their personal brand, even at the expense of the gravity created by others. They usually bring drama and react to office politics like the sky is falling. That's because politics are an opportunity to indulge their power and steal even more gravity.

Once you're a Shot Caller, the best way to handle a gravity stealer is to challenge their assertions. Ask "Where's your data?" Say "Please explain your logic." I've pushed back (hard) against gravity stealers, which ultimately led to my firing more than once. Who cares? Gravity stealers suck. Don't do it, and don't tolerate it.

For anyone in sales reading this, let me be clear about the "take your boss on the road" exercise that happens every day. Introducing your prospect to the boss is a good move if and only if the boss brings net new gravity to the call. That means their position at the company makes the customer feel superior about doing business together. Often, this requires nothing more than the boss being present and letting the salesperson accrue most of the goodwill from the call. It does *not* mean the boss does all the talking. Bringing your boss to a sales call also means removing fear from the mind of the sales professional. Any learning or coaching needs to be done in a positive fashion. If you manage salespeople and feel the need to "ride along" to audit the team, you've done a bad job on your shots. Blame yourself, not the salesperson.

KPI Till We Die

Key performance indicators are the biggest joke in business because Kabuki Dancers abuse them. Imagine this: A marathon runner is wearing a Fitbit to monitor their heart rate, steps, and run time. Based on that real-time observable data, the runner could adjust during the race and improve their performance. Sounds good. Now imagine the runner has a team of people staring at that same data and projecting that they will lose the race. What happens?

"Hey! You're not going fast enough. Run faster!" yells the team.

"I'm running as fast as I can!"

Then the fun starts. Only two things can happen next. One, everyone believes the runner is a world-class athlete who for some reason wasn't performing up to their potential. The team measures their oxygen intake, blood work, mental state, body mass index, sleep patterns, and on and on. Something must be wrong because God knows it can't be that we don't have a world-class runner on our team. The measuring goes on and on, the data comes back, and none of it moves the needle.

The second option is you don't have a world class performer on your team. No amount of measuring "what's wrong" will change that. But this never stops Kabuki Dancers from trying. That's the problem with misguided KPI tracking—it's almost always an attempt to find what isn't there.

In all my years under the performance microscope, I never benefited from some KPI revealing a way to adjust my performance. Most of the time, KPIs are used to find someone to blame for losing the race. If you're being "KPI'ed to death," the best response is to insist that everyone fix the why, not the who. That means studying your shots, figuring out why you missed, and correcting it. Your Whole Shot Grid should contain the KPIs or OKRs that matter. And all of your performance deficits can be identified using Shot Calling.

All Hat, No Cattle

"All sizzle, no steak." "All bark, no bite." "All Kabuki, no shots." We've all heard one of these expressions. I just added another.

"All hat, no cattle" refers to the person with no substance to add. Unlike gravity stealers, this Kabuki Dancer is trying to create gravity. Unfortunately, their contribution is to point out what's wrong without constructive feedback on how to fix it.

You'll notice this tell when you ask someone to describe their strategy to go from the current state to the desired state. If all they do is whine that the desired state hasn't been reached, they're Kabuki dancing. We all have to take this test, including me. That's why I use the current state, desired state approach—the framework forces you to call your shots. Use it.

Even if you're not the boss, not a team leader, or not an MBA grad, you can experience the power of structure-process-people-tools-incentives as the foundation of *your* suggestions on how to make progress. Consider this Shot-Calling practice. You and your career will benefit immensely.

One caution. Don't let all hat, no cattle become part of your personal brand. It will permanently limit your potential. When I start a new role, I promise myself, *Make your mark*. For better or worse, people should know what stamp you put on the endeavor. Shot calling isn't safe; it comes with risk. You can minimize that risk with the parameters I've laid out for you.

However, if you don't feel like your shots are creating healthy tension, you haven't gone far enough with imaging how awesome the desired state could be if everyone does their part. Tension management is critical here, so pay close attention to whether anything you say or do might create noise—and avoid it at all costs. I love the expression, "Anyone who says they never had a chance, never took a chance." It's true. It's time. Take risks. Call your shots. Step up your game. Win.

The Wizard Behind the Curtain

A company's curtain gets pulled back, and oh shit! There's a Kabuki Dancer pulling all the levers. They don't talk or act like a Kabuki Dancer. They might even be well liked. Hell, the business might be growing, and it seems like this person had a lot to do with it. Remember this: adversity doesn't create character, it reveals it. It's easy as pie to be amazing when everyone is winning. The real test happens when you're not. When mass is low, proximity is not bringing customers into orbit, and opposing gravity is eating you like a black hole. Then what?

My phone rings; that's what happens next. Someone got fired because that's what leaders do when the winning slows or stops. Then the search is on for someone who can turn the winning back on. I'm not the only person these companies call, but I get recruited often. For instance, the day I wrote this chapter, June 4, 2020, I had two calls. One was with the CEO of a Sequoia Ventures–backed company considered the hottest in their portfolio. The other was an executive recruiter from one of the most prestigious tech companies on the planet, with a market cap of over $150 billion. I took neither job. I'm more interested in helping you than helping them. Both interviews turned into conversations about Shot Calling. I made it clear that I don't sit behind the curtain and hope. I explained everything you've read in this book. On both calls, I heard, "Holy shit, we need you." That's what happens when you become a Shot Caller.

By the way, both gigs were worth $10 million minimum over the next two to four years, possibly way more and for longer. I turned them down for you. Learn this stuff. So one day, you'll be the one turning down $10 million job offers.

THE WHOLE SHOT

Near the end of my Trend Micro tenure, I held a planning meeting with my eleven direct reports, whose titles ranged from director to VP. Our purpose was to set targets for the year, so the meeting was important to everyone in the room. So important that ten minutes in, everyone had their laptop open checking email. *What the hell?* I needed their attention for one day. These targets drove our compensation for the year. Everyone had skin in the game, yet they were not engaging the way they needed to.

"I'd like you to listen," I said. "I'm looking for input on our upcoming year and feedback on how we can best achieve our targets. I'll capture everyone's suggestions. At the end of the meeting, let's evaluate them and rank them from best to worst. The person with the least number of valid suggestions at the end of the meeting is fired."

Hello. Eyes up, laptops shut. For better or worse, suggestions came. Of course, I had no intention of firing anyone. I wanted to make the point that nothing in their damn inbox was more important than that meeting.

I've thought about why I had to make an idle threat. Why would anyone in a meeting that could advance their career and make them a lot of money sit there and do email? It pissed me off until I realized it wasn't their fault. We had no system to guide us through all the interconnected facets of our business. They were never a part of creating anything resembling a Moonshot or any other shot for that matter. They were cut off from everything except their job titles and their teams. How could I expect them to add anything meaningful if they had no hand elsewhere in the business? Their only real opportunity to contribute was to guess and hope they didn't look foolish. Might as well hide behind email.

Now imagine that same planning meeting if they had all participated in creating the first four shots. No way they'd play it safe. On the contrary, they'd fight to get their ideas into the plan because of their emotional investment in those ideas. That's what the Whole Shot is: a forum for capturing all the ideas from the first four shots. By now you have completed the other four. It's time to square up to the basket and call your shot.

There is no difference between the Whole Shot and any planning process you've experienced before. Except everything leading up to it. At Trend Micro, we called our process "interlock." It wasn't bad, it just wasn't based on Shot Calling, so many important concepts were absent. The vast majority of the company was completely oblivious to interlock's purpose. Unless the few executives running the process got it right, the whole company would suffer.

Let's look at the essential elements for any operating plan and give them the Shot-Caller spin. Honestly, you could staple the first four shots together and be done with it. Just make sure your plan includes these additional components.

The Whole Shot Grid

Getting everyone on the same page is by far the most valuable consequence of Shot Calling. I've heard the lament about not being on the same page a thousand times. This process solves it. For good. The Whole Shot Grid also contains the very essence of Shot Calling because it requires you to set targets for everything. Every CEO who can have their teams produce a Whole Shot Grid has a blueprint for success. All they have to do is manage to the grid, and they win. If anything goes wrong, the blueprint tells you what to fix. Involve your whole company in this process if possible and share the grid when done. Create Shot

Callers, hold them accountable, and you become unstoppable. Here's a sample grid with guidance for each section.

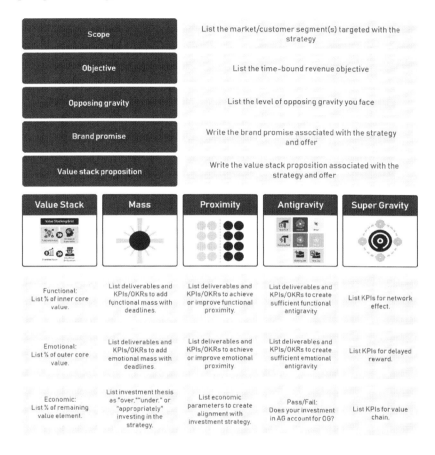

Figure 5 The Whole Shot Grid 2.0

Operating Plan Essentials

Let's spend some time on your operating plan components. These plans are ubiquitous across industries, but modify yours if anything is missing. The key to any operating plan is that you use it. Unfortunately, most sit in a drawer. It's not hard to figure out why. They don't help if there isn't a connection between the operating plan and each part of the business. Shot calling establishes that connection. It's better to have a brief, lightweight description of the four shots than some hundred-page plan that checks a bunch of perfunctory boxes.

Executive Summary

Start your plan with your Moonshot and Kill Shot deliverables: vision, mission, scope, objective, opposing gravity, brand promise, and value stack proposition. Then list out key actions you will take to hit your objectives. The Whole Shot Grid should contain most of these. Also, provide commentary on your logic behind these strategies, including your economic strategy in terms of over-, under-, or appropriately serving the market.

I always include commentary on risks the organization faces, but please don't put "failure to execute" as a risk. That misses the point of this whole damn book. Risk statements speak to inconsistencies between the shots that went unresolved during the planning process as well as macro conditions outside your control, including the simple risk of poor timing. Ultimately, any shortcomings will manifest in failing the Three *R*s Test, so describe any risk in those terms as well. Also include your confidence level in hitting the plan objectives. If it's not above 90 percent, you're not calling any shots. You're Kabuki dancing. Keep the Executive Summary to no more than three pages if possible.

Functional Sections

From here, your plan flows into a conventional construct that more or less mirrors your operating structure: innovation, engineering, and product strategies that are at the heart of value creation. This maps to the

Moonshot. In this section, flesh out your product roadmap. Express investments in terms of adding mass and describe your mass type—functional, emotional, or economic. The targets that measure the success of these investments should've been captured on your Whole Shot Grid, so make sure there are no discrepancies.

Risk statements in this section must be brutally honest. Flawed or delayed innovation strategies hurt everyone. This is the greatest risk to any business, so the CEO must be held accountable to mitigate that risk. Most of the time, such failure is laid at the feet of sales and marketing leadership. They belong at engineering or product's door. You can bullshit yourself about innovation risk, but you can't bullshit the market. Any executive, investor, or board member who can't act when they see this unfolding is not doing their job.

Marketing and all go-to-market strategies (proximity moves) maps to the Kill Shot. Your SAVE plan should account for all of these. Add market scope and competition commentary if necessary. Marketing leaders should be in lockstep with sales in terms of targets. Both should align with the CFO or financial plan owner as well. Express risk in terms of the Three Rs Test. If you fear you can't rationalize functional value, game over, so call it out. The same holds true for resolving emotional needs and reaffirming economic value. Do not sit on the fence. It's far better to fix the "why" because if you don't, someone is going to fix the "who." That means you!

Sales and channel strategies (proximity moves) are aligned to the Money Shot. Same deal as the Kill Shot—you should already have those strategies accounted for, including revenue targets and KPIs. Depending on your leadership role, you may need to account for performance-related investments here, including sales enablement or leadership development. Otherwise, you include those investments in the personnel investments section. Either way, those strategies match the Three-Point Shot.

Supporting Sections

So many great people work in Finance, HR, IT, Legal, and other supporting structures yet are not involved in operations planning. Let's change that. Any operating plan section related to these functions should align with the Moonshot and the Whole Shot Grid. Here's how.

1. **Hold the economic strategy line**. For instance, it's different for a finance team to manage an appropriately served strategy than one intended to overserve the market. Overserving a market means growth chasing. Other functions like Legal and HR also behave differently given a company's economic strategy. That's why *everyone* should become Shot Callers and participate in the planning process.

   Risk should be expressed by these functions in resource terms. You will fail if you don't have the resources to get the job done. Just like marketing leadership needs to call out risk with the Three *R*s Test, if resource constraints put you at considerable risk, call that out. One caution: be damn sure you need resources before declaring you can't succeed without them. There's an old Silicon Valley expression that "more companies die of indigestion than starvation." Don't get drunk on more resources and more tools. The test of a true Shot Caller is getting the job done with the *right* resources. Not more, not less. The right amount.

2. **Provide for operational effectiveness**. To run a tight ship, you have to do a lot right and in order. So why do many companies fail to execute? Is it because they didn't have the people, knowledge, or skill to deliver what was asked? Or was the request ambiguous? Unless Shot Callers are in charge, it's the latter. That's another reason *everyone* needs to be a Shot Caller; *everyone* needs to be involved in the planning process. Your operating plan should never be vague. It should be concise. And it will be—if you follow Shot Calling. Once you clarify exactly what

needs to be done, success is a function of getting out of people's way.

The financial section of any operating plan is straightforward. It contains P&L statements, cash positions, and burn rates. Any financial person has this covered. The key is to align with the market serving strategy in terms of over-, under-, or appropriately serving it. It drives me crazy when the strategy calls for growth and investment, yet the CFO nickels and dimes every decision. It's one thing to be financially responsible. It's another thing to be irresponsibly unaligned with strategy.

That's it, the essence of the Whole Shot is to do the other shots first! Once you learn how to do the other four shots, pulling them together is straightforward. A tremendously comprehensive plan based on Kabuki dancing will fail every time compared to an adequately written plan based on Shot Calling.

SHOT CALLING FOREVER: A BRIEF SUMMARY

Let's walk through the steps that once mastered will turn you into a Shot Caller. I was asked by a leading investment bank to consult for a company they just invested in. I'll leave the names out, but it's a huge opportunity capable of unicorn status. I'll help this company in many ways, and all of them are included in this sequence and are described in this book. The investor and CEO are both aware of *Call Your Shots* and are basically a living case study for the Shot-Caller system. Here's the sequence:

1. Learn about the reality of value creation and value types. Functional, emotional, and economic value are in play anytime humans exchange value, and most of perceived value emanates from the inner and outer core of any offer.

2. Value puts a dent in the fabric of business and creates gravity consisting of mass, proximity, antigravity, and super gravity. Strategy is the art and science of knowing how to manipulate this gravity to maximize your chance of achieving your objective.

3. Vision and mission are concepts that anchor your strategy to the big picture and account for your aspirational good and committed endeavor. Breakdowns in strategy and execution will eventually reveal themselves as vision or mission failures.

4. Bringing value, gravity, and strategy together requires an understanding of:

    a. Opposing gravity—the force holding your target customer in place and how to respond to that force.
    b. Inner core value—the value type created by your superpowers.
    c. Value stacking—the right way to position your offer so the majority of its value is revealed for maximum effect.
    d. Three *R*s Test—use this to understand what's working and what needs adjusting.

5. Set your objective, identify your target customer, and start preparing to create your Whole Shot Grid.

6. Understand value and strategy traps and how to avoid them.

7. Create your brand promise statement focused on inner core value.

8. Position the rest of your value by creating your value stack proposition.

9. Capture and integrate your proximity moves through your SAVE plan.

10. Model your performance expectations and assumptions.

11. Design your strategy for playing the symbols game effectively.

12. Bring your offer into the market and enable your sellers to sell at the highest level of strategic intersection, Level 3 selling.

13. Use the Three *R*s Test Cheat Sheet to dissect performance and adjust your Moonshot and Kill Shot until you pass the Three *R*s Test.

14. Find your leadership purpose and:

    a. lead authentically using leadership to connect with Shot Calling,
    b. manage tension and change effectively, and
    c. avoid being a Kabuki Dancer and refuse to allow anyone to be a mass-hole.

15. Bind everything together as through your Whole Shot.

I wrote this book to be your go-to resource for advancing your career and winning more. I recently told a friend that I don't really use my brain anymore in a business context. I just turn to the page in my book that addresses the situation at hand and apply the Shot-Calling System to deal with it.

But I have another motivation for writing this book. It's because of the pain I kept seeing and experiencing, especially in Silicon Valley. All the failure, criticism, stress, anger, bias, firings, and abuses going on all around me. Highly driven people thrashing about, willing to make any sacrifice, often bullying their way to the top. Cutthroat attitudes that petrify most people into silence as abuses of power continue under the threat of career annihilation. It's no wonder we hear the constant plea from people who simply want their voice to be heard. It's a relief actually to know that there's a system I can rely on to create a safe way for my ideas to be shared and my voice to be heard. I don't have to be afraid of sounding stupid or being dismissed by a Kabuki Dancer. I'm even empowered to push back against abuses of power that reduce gravity, and I have already told more than one person to "stop being a mass-hole!"

That's the power of a proven system. Anyone who learns it is *automatically* empowered because it works. That's why highly systems driven organizations like the military did a better job than business at integrating minorities and women. The system empowered them and they took advantage of it. We now have our first female NFL coach, Katie Sowers. She didn't get that job because she was an expert in playing football. She got the job because she became an expert in teaching football using a system. The 49ers hired her based on a job description, not a person description. That's what allowed them to look past the person and at the person's ability to do the damn job. Systems democratize power, plain and simple.

I am a huge fan of the show called *Bloomberg Technology*, hosted by Emily Chang. She is brilliant, talented, and fearless. She shook up Silicon Valley with her book *Brotopia*, which pointed out the massive inequities in women's participation in the valley, from executive roles, funding opportunities, and the unfair treatment women endure. She wants to help make it better, and so do I. If I ever get the chance to be interviewed by her, I'd tell her that in reality, most of these jobs aren't that hard. I'm not saying anyone could do every job, but other than skilled roles like engineering, someone who's underrepresented could do most of these jobs well if they had a system to lean on. Seriously, how hard is it to learn the fifteen steps outlined in the summary? Can you see yourself discussing gravity, mass, strategy, or brand promise statements in a meeting, feeling like you have something to say? Of course you can, once you're a Shot Caller!

I'll leave you with this. Here's my vision, or aspirational good, for the Shot-Calling System:

A business world where gravity guides decisions, promises made are promises kept, authenticity triumphs over fear, and Shot Callers replace Kabuki Dancers.

So become a Shot Caller, and let's make this reality. Thanks very much!

ACKNOWLEDGMENTS

This book would not have been possible without the help, support, friendship, and contribution of many people: My family, Laura, Kate, and Thomas and my parents Irene and Bob. And the many others, in no particular order, that include, but are certainly not limited to: Brian Harmon, Brian Henger, Mahbod Seraji, Teresa Nepa, Jim Phee, Peter Brownell, Scott Bacarella, Roger Cobb, Al Collins, Frank Walsh, Brendan Fitzgerald, Monty Venkersammy, Joe Coglitore, Lane Bess, Carol Carpenter, John Maddison, Steve Quane, Punit Minocha, Susan Orbuch, Dan Woodward, Eva Chen, Raimund Genes, Steve Chang, Mahendra Negi, Anthony O'Mara, Mike Gable, Dave Patniak, David Twilley, Michelle Denman, Shawn and Samantha Murphy, Vince Kearns, Robert Munne, Dinesh Rau, Mike Lesick, RJ Singh, Rob and Rich Boylan, Gene Jozwiak, Tom Preiss, Steve Spadaccini, Ron Clarkson, Robert Liu, Dave Lieberman, Ken Beer, Maureen McCormick, Derek Goggin, Ed Brown, Mike Williams, Kyle and Misty Chandler, Bill Dolby, Dan Glessner, and all the other cool people at Trend Micro, Chenxi Wang, CJ Patella, Rebecca Kline, Mark Patton, Marcin Kleczynski, Pedro Bustamante, Mark Harris, Fernando Francisco, Aric Bendorf, Analisa Travaglione, David Ho, Jeff Hurmuses and all the cool people at Malwarebytes, Steven Watson, Atiq Raza, Dave Furneaux, Satya Gupta and all the cool people at Virsec, Anthony Ulwick, Eric Eskey, Dave DeWalt, Anthony Enrico, Chantz Oliver, and all the cool people at Emailage, Tamer Hassan, Michael Tiffany, and all the cool people at White Ops.

GLOSSARY

Antigravity	Strategies designed specifically to offset opposing gravity use antigravity to defeat opposing gravity.
Brand Promise Statement	The concise description of the unique promise of worthiness associated with your offer's inner core.
Delayed Reward	A form of super gravity that occurs when an offer is seeded throughout the marketplace to monetize at a later point.
Gravity	The force in business that determines how markets take form and organize.
Kabuki Dancer	Anyone who guesses what works in business and why.
Kill Shot	The shot that addresses brand promise, value stack proposition, packaging, and the SAVE framework.
Mass	The foundation for creating gravity based on your core's value. The bigger and more valuable your core is, the more mass your offer has. Ideally, you want "mass out the ass."
Mission	A statement indicating the "committed endeavor" that connects your inner core and your strategy.
Money Shot	The shot that describes the best way to win in sales.
Moonshot	The shot that addresses value creation and strategy.
Network Effect	A form of super gravity that occurs when participants in the consumption of an offer automatically create more participants through their use of the offer.

Opposing Gravity	The force exerted against your offer coming from alternatives to your offer, including the biggest source of gravity in the universe, the status quo.
Orbit	The condition that exists when your strategy is working as designed and you have achieved your desired level of balance with the marketplace.
Proximity	A way to increase your overall gravity by bringing your mass close to the target customer.
SAVE	An acronym that replaces the "Four *P*s" of marketing: solution, access, value, educate.
Shot Caller	Anyone who learns how to take and make all five shots: Moonshot, Kill Shot, Money Shot, Three-Point Shot, Whole Shot.
Super Gravity	Strategies that increase gravity disproportionately to the resource expended can create super gravity.
Three-Point Shot	The shot that recommends the best way to lead people, manage tension, handle change, and unify teams.
The Three *R*s Test	A simple framework to understand if your offer will succeed, determined by whether you can rationalize functional value, resolve emotional value, and reinforce economic value.
Value	The reason customers buy, which they perceive as functional value, emotional value, economic value, or some combination of all three, with one form of value taking priority in the transaction.
Value Chain	A form of super gravity where the exchange of value between participants is prearranged and the reward system dictated by the primary driver of the value chain.
Value Stack Proposition	The full description of your offer's inner core, outer core and mantle layers of value—functional, emotional, or economic value.
Vision	A statement indicating the "aspirational good" your company seeks to deliver.
Whole Shot	The shot that describes how to bring together all the shots into a single coherent plan.

THE SHOT CALLER'S READING LIST

What Customers Want: Using Outcome-Driven Innovation to Create Breakthrough Products and Services by Anthony W. Ulwick

Dealing with Darwin: How Great Companies Innovate at Every Phase of Their Evolution Paperback by Geoffrey A. Moore

The Challenger Sale: Taking Control of the Customer Conversation by Matthew Dixon and Brent Adamson

True North: Discover Your Authentic Leadership by Bill George and Peter Eagle Sims

ABOUT THE AUTHOR

Thomas J. Miller is a world-class cybersecurity executive and alumnus of Trend Micro, Malwarebytes, and Zscaler. For over thirty-five years, Tom has led sales, marketing, product management, and P&L growth for both public corporations and startups. He has repeatedly led companies through industry IT inflection points, has created scalable go-to-market strategies, and has successfully managed enterprise-wide transformations. Tom's achievements include:

- Leading all sales, channel, business development, e-commerce, retail, service provider strategy and go-to-market activity at a high-velocity security company, spanning enterprise, SMB, and consumer security solutions, resulting in 400+ percent growth in three years and a 5x valuation increase in eighteen months.
- Driving strategic planning and M&A development, all US go-to-market strategy, sales and marketing operations, and key growth initiatives with established industry players. One roadmap resulted in this segment going from -10 percent YoY growth to +25 percent.
- Delivering 70 percent growth every year, more than 2x the industry growth rate.
- Receiving 14 Presidents Club Awards, 3 Chairman's Club Awards, and 3 Sales Rep of the Year Awards.
- Participating in three successful IPOs driven by key customer successes.
- Completing 50+ weeks of postgraduate professional education/ training.

Tom's first book, *Call Your Shots: A Uniquely Workable Approach for Demystifying the Universal Laws of Business, Creating Winning Strategy, Unlocking Value, Unifying Teams, Avoiding Peril, and Making You Unstoppable*, teaches business professionals in any role or industry how to earn a seat at the table, get everyone on the same page, and become a Shot Caller—someone who sets and hits targets in the five core business areas of strategy, marketing, sales, performance, and operations. Create a culture of Shot Callers at www.ShotCallerSystem.com.

Printed in Great Britain
by Amazon